Journey through Organization Theory

dr. J. Polling

prof. drs. A. A. Kampfraath

Table of Contents

Preface

The Need for a Timestamp

This is a book about change in organization theory in and by a changing environment. That is, it is not the theory itself that is our concern but its change over time and the factors in the social environment that cause the theory to change.

That organization theory changes will surprise nobody and that our environment changes is just as obvious. But where both – organization theory and environment – change over time any book on organization theory should be dated. People should be able to know when and where and under what conditions the book was written. It is customary to date a book by putting a copyright year on it. But only putting a year – say 1980 – in your book doesn't say very much about the situation, the constraints or the environment that were relevant for organizations at the time. When we see that '*In Search of Excellence*' was published in 1980 do we in 2015 realize that this was the same year that Ronald Reagan was elected president of the US and announced a new economic program?

As conditions seem to change ever faster it gets more and more difficult to look at events in their proper perspective and see them as contemporaries would have seen them. That is why we decided to date this book with – be it very short and sober – a picture of our world as we see it now. That is what this preface is about; we try to give this book a date – a timestamp. We do that by using the environmental factors that will reappear in the subsequent chapters of this book. So we have a look at markets and institutions, at technical and economical elements and at the culture in organizations and in society.

Changing Market Conditions

Our world then is dominated by change on a global scale. Even since 2007 – the year this text was first published – many things have changed. 2007 was just before the biggest financial and economic crisis since 1930 occurred. The crisis coincided or maybe even stimulated the slow shift of the economic point of gravity from West to East. Not everybody is happy with those structural changes. A number of writers express their concern about the loss of Western dominance and superiority. (see for instance: Huffington, Krugman, Mojo, Stiglitz).

China and India show growth percentages far above those of the west. With a percentage of about 5% China can be seen as the real push behind globalization. And with a population of more than 1.3 billion people, the country is seen as much as a challenge as it is a threat. Big investors not only see China as a big market for their sought for products. Though China is losing its position as a reservoir of cheap labor, for international operating enterprises it is still very attractive for outsourcing their production. From 2004, even a typical American company as Levi's has moved its entire production to China. As a result of the enormous production capacity of China, markets in Western Europe and the United States are flooded with cheap Chinese products. This happens at the expense of the competitive position of the West and will result in the loss of millions of jobs, unless the western countries are able to reinvent themselves.

But while China may be the most conspicuous of the competing new countries, India is following close behind and most countries in Africa are fast growing also.

Changing the Institutional Background

Among the institutional factors that determine the shift in market positions are the democratic character of the governments of the competing countries. Private property and the rule of law in democratic reigned countries seem to give better possibilities of sustainable growth. In this respect India might have better opportunities in the long run then China. But for the countries of the West (Europe and maybe to a lesser extent the Unites States) to keep their competitive power it seems inevitable to implement structural change in labor relations. We are witness to the strenuous processes that accompany the adjustments in which government, business and labor unions are looking for and trying out new relations.

On the level of global international institutions the now ongoing negociations around TIPP and TISA probably will govern our international trade relations for years to come.

The institutional background is largely influenced by the political conflicts we are witness off now. The situation in the Middle East that generates millions of migrants towards Europe gives in the European countries new questions around border control, while in the mean time Russian actions give reminiscences of a reliving cold war.

Changing Technology

Technological change and innovation have always been the engine for economical development and growth. But maybe never before was technology so pervasive in every direction we look as during the last century. Already around 1980 Toffler mentioned the powershift consequences of the post industrial society. Since about 2000 practically everybody on this planet is interconnected through the internet. This has lead to unexpected results as the Arabian Spring. The internet opens also markets for new gigantic enterprises as Facebook, Google or Amazon. These companies among others are now competing for access to 'Big Data'. Under influence of the internet other companies are trying to reinvent there business to keep in contact with their consumers. The 'internet of things' gives possibilities for production on a scale we cannot yet oversee.

About this Book

This book, intended for students and interested layman, introduces organization theory from a perspective that gets little attention in most textbooks. We will show how organization theory is rooted in the development of its environment and of society. Therewith attention is drawn to the time-bound nature of its body of knowledge.

We have used many examples from developments in the Netherlands. This of course is a result of the history of this text which was first written in Dutch for a Dutch audience. But for this edition we kept this Dutch flavor because it showes at the same time how a small country in Western Europe follows international trends.

1. Introduction

The terms organization theory and management theory are indications of a field that most of the time is viewed as a collection of opinions - a body of knowledge - about organizations, about their structure, their functioning, and about the way their functioning can be improved. The term 'body of knowledge' is used because the knowledge about organizations has been collected from different disciplines throughout history, but does not always show a great coherence. One could say that at the bottom of the collected knowledge there is also a variety of paradigms.

Moreover we find opinions about organizations under different names. We speak of organization theory, organization science, or management theory. It all depends on the emphasis that contributors to the theory want to stress. We will leave the discussion about the scientific status of this field alone. In chapter 6 however we will look at a few aspects of the theory in more detail.

When we look at the literature on organization theory we feel that hardly anybody pays any attention to the historical conditions under which theories were brought forward. That in itself should not surprise us very much. An important part of the material on which the theory is built was collected in studies in which a large number of organizations were compared at a certain point in time. Apparently those organizations worked under the same historical conditions that were known to both contributors and readers. There was no need to mention them explicitly. But when we take a closer look at the different studies, we will see that the contributors were not always aware how much their opinions and statements were influenced by their environment and by the time in which they lived. Therefore, it is not always clear under what conditions the different theories must be thought valid.

In this book we focus our attention on the historical conditions. We will show that the different opinions and contributions that make up the body of knowledge of organization theory did not come out of nowhere, but that they are in more than one way a product of their times. Changes in theory have their roots in the changing environment where organizations operated and contributors made their contributions.

Or when we look at it from the other side, we should see that if conditions change enough, existing theory loses part of its validity. We will use a major part of this book – the chapters 3, 4 and 5 – to look at the relationship between theory and environment.

In history we find many references towards organizational principles – for instance, some people say that Jethro, Moses' father in law, was the first management consultant in history and, as a matter of fact, the principles Jethro used sound familiar enough even today.

But there is ample reason to start the history of organization theory at the end of the 19th century. Around that time Taylor gave the first consistent synopsis of organizational problems, while his contemporary, Fayol, is seen as the first who distinguished management as a separate task in the organization. In chapter 3 we will examine the factors that caused their theories to be formulated in that time and in that way.

The title of chapter 3 - Classical Organization Theory – must be seen not only as a way of thinking about organizations. It is used at the same time to delineate a period that lasted from about 1910 until about 1950.

In chapter 4, we find ourselves about thirty years later. Circumstances had changed considerably since the days of Taylor and Fayol. New studies of organizations carried traces of this change. They introduced a new way of thinking about managing organizations which in this book is called "Socio-technical Management." This term "Socio-technical Management" is also used here to both designate a way of thinking and to distinguish a period that lasted more or less from 1940 till about 1970.

In the next chapter (5) we see that around 1970 conditions had changed again. There was need for new theory. We called this chapter Contingency Management after one of the important streams after 1960. In this period we see a growing interest for the environment of organizations.

Points of Attention
It is clear that the periods indicated have a certain overlap. We must realize that the chronological sequence of periods as indicated here is somehow arbitrary. In real life one school of thought is not suddenly replaced by another. New points of view only break through in literature and in practice gradually until they become the dominant theory. But even then many views and opinions from the past remain important and actual.

Though we will discuss in the chapters 3, 4 and 5, several organization theories at some length this book is not meant to present an outline of the history of organizational theory. The theories that appear in these chapters – though characteristic of their times – are selected primarily to illustrate the relationship between theory and environment. That environment was in most situations geographically determined. The situation in the United States was totally different from that in the Netherlands or France. Therefore, we travel in this book not only from theory to theory but also from country to country. Our selection can rightly be seen as a journey through theory, as much a journey through time and as a trip through different countries. But before we embark on our voyage we'll try and explain in chapter 2 our starting point and the reasons for our approach.

It shouldn't surprise the reader that most of the theories and examples are drawn from theories and developments in the United States. The period in which the organization theory started coincided with the time the United States took over the position as biggest economic power from Great Britain. The fast growth of the United States was also the cause that many of the developments in theory were conceived there for the first time and became the lead for developments and opinions in other industrialized countries.

In chapter 6 we will look in more detail at a few characteristics of theory building in organization theory. They may give us a possible explanation for the handicaps that inhibit further development of the theory. In chapter 7 we will show how, under the influence of the existing constraints and environmental factors, the focus of organization theory changes. And in chapter 8 we will see whether the insight we got can help us with further development of the theory.

2. Organizations and Organization Theory

Organizations

Some things are so obvious that hardly anybody looks at them twice. So it is nearly self-evident that people are different in talents and in skills. We see thinkers and doers, hunters and farmers, carpenters, stone-cutters and smiths, and leaders and followers. Differentiation in human societies is as old as human society itself. Just as obvious is the phenomenon that people form groups and organizations to do tasks together for which their individual qualities, knowledge and/or means are insufficient. From the earliest times on, there are reports on more or less large organizations. The accomplishments of these organizations still fascinate us and fill us with amazement. Large buildings from the past such as the Egyptian pyramids or the British constructions of megaliths still lead to the question: how were these constructions built, how was the work to build them organized?

These are questions of modern man from the western hemisphere. Modern man who lives in a world that is accustomed to large and still larger organizations that permeate our society in all directions. It is a world in which we are accustomed to using large equipment for projects in which large quantities of material have to be moved. But how did man realize these jobs at the dawn of our civilization? What methods did he use, what tools were available to him?

Organization of Cooperation

Organizations are so obvious that one can sympathize with

March and Simon[1] when they say that many of our opinions about organizations don't rise above the level of common sense and have hardly any scientific background. We also agree with them that - to improve our knowledge of organizations and eventually be able to pass it on to others – we must express ourselves as accurately as possible.

Organizations, it's true, are groups of people but not every group of people can be called an organization. We see an organization as a cooperation of people directed toward the achievement of one or more goals.

When we look at an organization in more detail we see in every organization a leader (a manager) who induces those who are led (employees) to give their contribution to achieve the goals. This leader organizes the cooperation. We see this elementary picture regardless the size of the organization. In large organizations – we call them large because the number of employees is large - the task of the leader has expanded and his function has grown into a complex governing organ. In some cases we also see how in this governing organ specialization takes place; we see an organ that is occupied with current affairs and another organ that supervises and checks and adjusts where necessary.
This image of a management that organizes cooperation and gives instructions to employees who execute the commands is universal. We find it in private corporations and in government organizations. In government the management has got the form of a political governing organ. In local government, for instance, we see the municipal executive as responsible for management and organization, while policy and control are in the hands of the council.

---

1   March and Simon, 1969.

People (Managers and Employees)

The way in which the cooperation in an organization is realized draws our attention immediately to the relationship between the leader and his employees. This relationship is of crucial importance for the possibilities of the leader to realize his goals and also for the requirements that are imposed on his leadership. But the requirements for the leader depend also on the qualities of his employees. In organizations with many highly specialized professionals, (sometimes as is the case in hospitals with their own professional ethics), the leader knows in general not enough of the work content to influence it directly. This creates a separate issue that occupied many writers on organizations in the sixties of the 20th century. Kampfraath[2] pointed out that in these cases the role of the manager is strongly directed towards creating conditions that make cooperation possible. Etzioni goes even further and suggests that in certain types of organizations, such as research laboratoria, hospitals and universities, the roles of staff and line are reversed.[3]

We will see that this element – the relationship between the leader (the manager) on one side and those who are led (employees) on the other side – is a recurring issue in the theory of organizations. Much of the discussion in recent theory is about personal qualities (like empathy, communicative skills, etc.) and the kind of knowledge a leader should have (structuring of the organization, planning of activities, financial knowledge and knowledge of the most important primary processes). Nowadays much emphasis is put on the role of a manager as a coach for his employees.

---

2   Kampfraath, 1969.
3   Kast, 1974, 217.

Goals

The relationship between leader and employee is not the only recurrent theme in theory. Organizations are directed towards the realization of one or more goals. That is why many discussions on organizations are about the goals of the organization and the way in which they can be reached. Determining and realizing goals are from the beginning also a recurring element in the organization theory.

According to general economic theory the goal of the enterprise is profit maximization. As can be easily demonstrated, profit maximization is reached when marginal costs equal marginal returns. Though theoretically sound, this hypothesis was not usable in practice.[4] We share in this the opinion of Drucker[5] when he says that profit doesn't give an explanation for the behavior and decisions of the entrepreneur, but acts as a touchstone for their soundness.

A survey of the discussion around organizational goals is found in Mintzberg (1983). His survey is part of his introduction to power in and around organizations. His review ends with the opinion of Georgiou who says that the enterprise has no goal at all. As we have defined the organization as a corporation with a goal, an opinion as that of Georgiou falls outside the scope of organization theory as we see it. In practice we see that in an organization several goals have to be achieved. To make progress in achieving those goals decisions have to be made on an ongoing basis.

---

4   See for instance Dopuch, 1974, 17.
5   Drucker, 1957.

Costs and Culture

Discussions about the goals of the organization draw attention to the fact that the performances of an organization cost money. The people that contribute to the work that has to be done have to be rewarded. The organization of the operational work, the way in which tasks are divided, machines and other resources that are employed, in short, work habits and work methods influence the costs. That is also a very obvious matter in a society in which money has come to be used as well as a means for exchange of goods, as a measure of value and as a unit for calculation.

Costs have to be compensated by the revenues of organizational performance. That puts some stress on the leader and the employees while achieving the goals of the organization. As we shall see the behavior of leader and employees towards each other cannot be without obligations. Towards his employees the leader possesses a position of power with two aspects. The manager is held responsible not only for his own performance but also for that of his employees. As a result of this he has to evaluate the performance of his employees and have the authority to sanction when necessary. At the same time the manager must stimulate the people in his department to deliver their performance to the best of their abilities.

Organizations are different; you could say they are unique like people are unique. The differences depend, among other things, on the size of the organization, their tasks or work processes and on the organizational culture. The organizational culture develops in relation to the people who are present in the organization. It is preserved because new employees adapt to the existing culture and those who don't feel at home will leave.

An Open System

But just like people organizations share a number of characteristics. We already mentioned several of these characteristics:
It is all about **people, working together, towards goals**. There
are leaders and employees, there is a division of labor and there
is an organizational culture. This means that there are questions
that are common to all kinds of organization. And that gives us
a basis for a scientific approach.

Though organizations are unique they are not alone. They have
to deal with other organizations, some of them in a competing
role and others as suppliers or customers. Moreover, they
operate in an environment that influences the organization in a
number of ways as shown in Fig. 1.

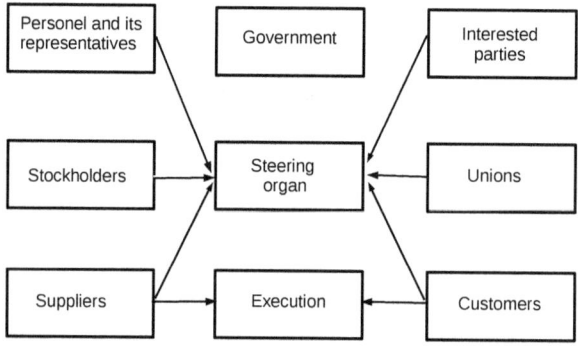

*Fig.1 Parties that have an interest in the organization
(stakeholders)*

In the next sections and also in the subsequent chapters we will
explore the environment of organizations in more detail.

The analogy between men and organizations wasn't mentioned by accident. It fits in a theory that was put forward in the middle of the twentieth century: systems theory, a theory in which a hierarchy of systems was suggested ranging from structures to transcendental. Since systems theory was introduced organizations are often seen as open systems. The elements of open systems are, according to Beer[6] dynamically linked in time. Systems approach shows us that relations in organizations can be very complex indeed. And yet we must realize that the system that is called organization is still a cooporation of people directed towards goals.

Organization Theory

In spite of the fact that organizations exist since time immemorial it seems that the interest in organizations as a phenomenon as such is something of the nineteenth century. In the beginning of the 19th century - in a time when the first effects of the industrial revolution were felt - many observations were made on managing organizations by writers with different points of view. On the economic side we find material by writers like Adam Smith and David Ricardo. From a technical perspective Charles Babbage and James Watt expressed their views, whereas social aspects were tackled by people like Saint Simon and Karl Marx.

Body of Knowledge

The first systematic observations on governing and managing organizations didn't appear before the beginning of the 20th century (Taylor, Fayol). In the years following their publications many texts from very different points of view were dedicated to aspects of organization that seemed to complement

---

6   Beer, 1979.

each other or seemed to contradict each other. New opinions rose, others disappeared. New opinions often reacted against older views. Only seldom did the question arise under what conditions the theories were supposed to be working. There is hardly any systematic evaluation. As a consequence the views of different generations of organization experts remain unchallenged and stand side by side. The image of the organization theory that emerged was that of a patchwork quilt of views that could be best seen as a body of knowledge.

A number of writers has been dealing with the scientific quality of organization theory. For instance, March and Simon (1969) who try to test the scientific value of existing opinions, or Wilfred Brown[7] who argues in favor of a common standardized language as a basis for the organization theory. Their efforts seem to have had little success. People have not succeeded in building a solid science on organizations. It is a situation that seems to be accepted in our times. According to Pröpper[8], *The organization is a complex ever changing phenomenon and so not surprisingly we cannot speak of an unequivocal all comprising organization theory.*

The lack of agreement about the content of the organization theory opens the possibility for coming into being of 'private organization theories' (see also chapter 6). For though there is a mainstream of opinions that we will call 'the general organization theory', managers and organizations consultants can and will supplement the opinions from this mainstream with their own opinions. So we see that as a result of the special way in which the theory expands sometimes opinions remain in the general organization theory that must be regarded as out of date. Such opinions can survive just because there is no agreed on framework.

---

7   Brown, 1971.
8   Pröpper, 1993, 5.

Two Kinds of Problems

The notion that an organization can be seen as an open system in continuous interaction with its environment leads to two kinds of problems. On one hand questions arise about the limits of the system that is called organization. This not just an academic question. We have already seen that in the environment of the organization many institutions and parties try to influence what is going on inside. Stockholders try to influence things by means of the stockholder meetings; unions try to implement their opinions through their members: the employees in the organization; pressure groups bring about a moral climate around the organization (think of non-smoking campaigns, Greenpeace etc). From the environment there is a constant diffusion of opinions and views that affect the behavior of managers and employees in the organization. Besides that we see that recent concepts of networks and chains try to see the behavior of groups of organizations as that of links in a chain or as nodes in a network.

Moreover if we consider an organization as an open system we can distinguish a number of subsystems[9] each with its own boundaries. Do all these boundaries fall within the boundary of the system we call an organization? And is this still true if we look at the financial subsystem?[10]

What are the boundaries of the organization? Or: what is the object that organization theory is looking at? We defined an organization as a cooperation of people directed towards the achievement of one or more goals. Therefore we say that the borders of the organization are marked by the people that belong to the organization. And those people belong to the organization who appear on its payroll.

---

9   Kast, 1974, 112.
10 Kramer, 1991, 38.

On the other hand the question arises to what extent structure and functioning of the organization are influenced by the environment. This is a question that remarkably is not raised very often. Only a small number of studies - like those of Chandler (1962) of Burns and Stalker (1966) and following in their footsteps Lawrence and Lorsch[11] pointed at aspects of this influence. In chapter 6 we will address this issue again.

The Scientific Object of Organization Theory

Organizations as open systems in an environment and with many participants draw the attention of several disciplines. The views and findings of these disciplines have made an important contribution to the views in organization theory. As a result organization theory has got a multi-specialist nature. That brings the risk that we lose sight of the essence of organization theory and that - be it interesting - views are added that shouldn't be reckoned to belong to organization theory. We met already an example in the views of Georgiou.

What is organization theory about? What is its scientific object? What is the angle from which organization theory studies organizational phenomenon? The scientific object distinguishes the observations that belong to the organization theory from other observations about organizations. In this book we see the scientific object as: *the most efficient allocation of people and means to reach the goals of the organization.*

Starting from this scientific object organization theory occupies itself mainly with the following issues:

- structuring and functioning of organizations
- the application of techniques in organizations

---

11 Lawrence and Lorsch, 1967.

- the relations between the different participants that are involved in the organization;
- the steering, governing and control of activities in an organization;
- the problems concerning coordination and integration of the contributions of the different participants in an organization;
- the problems of strategy and tactics in planning the activities in an organization.

This could be called the domain of the organization theory.

Organization theories don't come into being without cause. They find their origin in the same environment that influenced the organization in the first place. To illustrate this we shall first deal to some extent with the environment and in the next chapters try to give an outline of the environment in which several theories came into being.

The Environment

We have already seen that many parties try to influence the organization. They are parties that in one way or another have an interest in the organization: or in the wording of our day, the stakeholders. The stakeholders are one element in the environment of the organization.

There are more factors that must be reckoned to the environment of an organization. Some of these factors are of a neutral non-personal nature. From the position of the leaders of the organization they can be seen as data. Data in the sense that the leaders have only little possibilities to change their effects. The fact however that they can hardly be influenced by the leaders doesn't mean they are constant over time. The environment changes. Considering the neutral and non-personal nature of these environmental factors it looks obvious that in a certain period and in a certain geographically territorial space, all or nearly all organizations will be confronted with the same environmental factors and their changes.

In the next pages we will direct our attention to just the changes in the environment. As a matter of fact it is plausible that change in environmental data will have their effect on organization theory. Therefore it is important to explore the environment a little further. We distinguish as environmental factors: markets, institutions, culture, science and technology and the economic climate.

Markets

Organizations operate between different markets. On the input side we see the markets for raw and other materials and the market for the means of production. On the output side we have the markets for intermediate and finished products.

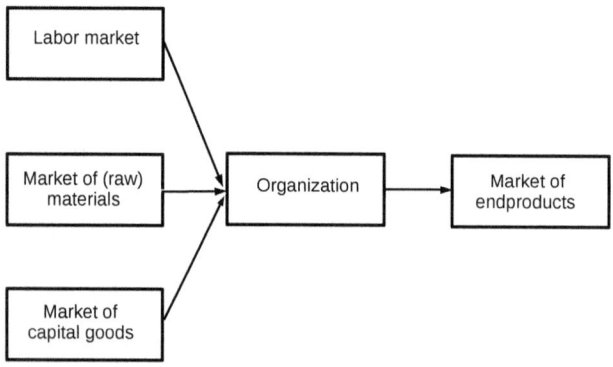

Fig. 2 Organization between markets

The situation on all of these markets has its bearing on the behaviour of the organization. A labor market in which certain kinds of labor are scarce has a tendency to raise wages. This may change wage differences and thereby create internal tension. An undisturbed flow of raw and other material is of the utmost importance for the continuance of an organization while the situation on the market of end products is the governing factor for the marketing strategy to be followed. The position of the organization can be drawn as in figure 2.

The situations on the different markets have economically short term and long term or structural characteristics. The long term characteristics of market conditions are important because they are a decisive factor in the choice of a place for our businesses, though it must be admitted that it was more important in the period of the industrial revolution than it is now. In that period industries had their domiciles where the raw materials were found. As traffic and transport got better the choice of a business place near the origin of the raw materials became less important. An analysis of Alfred Weber made in the years 20 of the 20th century showed that the choice of a business place was only determined by the costs of transport and the cost of labor.[12] Cost of transport in our days hardly influence the choice of business place. That means that the markets of (raw) materials of production and end products can be spread around the world, as they actually are. This is different for the costs of labor which are still determined by the situation on the local labor market. The structure of the labor market - the presence or availability of sufficient workers with suitable knowledge and capabilities - is still a major argument in decisions around the business place. The discussions around out-sourcing to countries with low wages gives us a good example.

---

12 Cited in Meij, 1958:252.

In chapter 3 we will see how the development of the leading industrialized countries was influenced by the structure of the markets of raw materials and the structural characteristics of the labor market (including the very different growth of the labor population). In chapter 8 we will look again at the changes in the structure of the labor market.

The position of the enterprise in a market not only determines the behavior of the entrepreneur but also the strategy he has to follow. The extent in which he can act as a monopolist - in the market of end products - determines his possibilities to influence the price of his product. The same is true for the markets of raw materials and means of production. The leader of an organization always seeks to at least maintain and, where possible, to better his position on the different markets.

An Institutional Framework

The whole set of laws around, for instance, labor relations, environmental care, technical and legal constraints have an important bearing on the position of the organization among other competing organizations and for the possibilities of an organization to maintain or better its market position. Brogan, for instance, shows that the accumulation of capital in the United States between 1865 and 1890 was possible because of the almost total absence of a framework in which entrepreneurs had to function or maybe because a situation existed in which entrepreneurs could ignore the existing rules.

Only during that period, which raced to apply modern techniques to the largely untouched resources of North America, was the need for massive capital investment so urgent and so difficult to satisfy adequately that the appetites of the capitalists, the money men, prevailed over all other social forces. In that age, laws and legal processes were altered, reinterpreted, perverted or ignored; the interests of working men and women were trampled upon; the appeal to the greed, foresight or gambler's instinct of the wealthy led to innumerable shady operations, the principles of political economy were reinvented and the interests of the consumer, the ultimate customer were for long ignored.[13]

This is in sharp contrast with an example about the slow development of the bread and flour production as a result of the Dutch laws and regulations in the 19th century:

Millers were not allowed to deal in flour or grain. they had to wait until the customers came to the mill, they were not allowed to bake bread and were obliged to handle each batch of grain separately, together with the tax documents that belonged to it. This made it impossible to organize a continuous production.[14]

But we don't have to go back in time that far. The current discussion about labor conditions, affordable retirement schemes or the suffocating rules show how much the entrepreneurs in Western-Europe feel themselves prisoners in this institutional framework.

Culture

Culture in an organization (the way in which managers and co-workers interact and treat each other) can - and generally will - differ from the culture in the environment. But when the difference gets too big tensions arise in the organization that require the organization to adapt. There is much agreement to the fact that the culture in a country as much as that in an organization is a fairly stable factor and difficult to change.[15] Hofstede distinguishes between the (stable) core of values and

---

13 Brogan, 1985, 392.
14 Luiten van Zanden, 2000, 178.
15 Hofstede, 1994, 9.

the more flexible practices of a culture. Shifts in the practices of a culture seem fairly well possible. Zahn says in relation to the events in the Netherlands between 1965 and 1975:

According to political criteria The Netherlands is a democracy. The existing political order, however, was characterized as 'structurally' unjust and as undemocratic (...). And this meant that 'the right' lost its legitimacy as a 'conservative alternative'. For if the existing society was structurally unjust and undemocratic there was nothing to conserve.[16]

This explains the broad resistance against power and authority in The Netherlands in the years 70 of the twentieth century. This period didn't last very long. Already about 1980 a return to more hierarchical relations had become obvious and was expressed in the no-nonsense policy of a new generation of magistrates. It is one of the tasks of the manager to interpret changes in culture in time and to incorporate them in his attitude towards his employees.

In the years between 1980 and 1990 it became clear that important differences exist between cultures of different organizations. But not only between organizations in one country; there are important differences in culture between countries also. Hofstede remarks that solutions that are used in France for structuring and arranging organizations differ from those used, for instance, in Great Britain or Germany. In his view this is in relation to the differences in culture between these countries.

Science and Technology

Development in science and technology are seen as the most important engines behind economic development. They make

---

16 Zahn, 1991, 19.

new markets possible and use new resources. Development means that existing products suffer from a fast form of aging although this is not true for all products alike. For the individual enterprise in a branch with quick changes it means that there are many insecurities about their own market position. In this context one might think of the developments in telecommunications. Developments force them to adjust their internal organization and their strategy regularly to keep up with competitors.

Developments in technology follow those in science. Among the sciences physics and chemistry rate very high together with biology. The fabulous success of science and technology not only caused their research methods to be an example for other disciplines it also influenced the views on society of nineteenth and early twentieth century man. It supported the idea that rational man could make society as he wished it. The social and behavioral sciences (economy, sociology, psychology) emerged and developed in this atmosphere of a man-made society. The results in the new disciplines however were not always very spectacular; partly because of the fact that experiments could not very easily be reproduced, partly because it proved difficult to develop a common language and a common paradigm for these sciences.

While results in the social sciences were not always unambiguous, their impact on the thinking about functioning and structuring of organizations was not less important than the influence of ideas that originated in the technical and economical disciplines.

The Economical Climate

As we will see, the growth of different industrial countries between 1850 and 1930 was very different. To accommodate the growth it was necessary to maintain a high level of investments. But high investments go at the expense of consumption which meant that wages of labor had to be kept low. In many of the old European countries there were institutions that prevented wages from dropping below a certain level as we have seen before, except for the new industries where no traditions existed for the level of pay.

The attention of economists in the nineteenth century was also drawn to the ups and downs in production and commerce - the economic trade cycles - that greatly influenced the behavior of entrepreneurs and the position of laborers. Periods of unemployment weaken the position of the laborers, while periods of high employment rates strengthen it.

The Environment at Work

In the next chapters we will see the environmental factors at work in creating a climate in which new theories can be formulated successfully. Successively we see how market conditions, institutions, economic development and cultural elements exercise their influence on existing theories and this against a background of ever faster changing available techniques and progression in science.

Our fundamental notion is that organization theories have their roots in the conditions that existed at the time they were formulated. So whenever a new theory is formulated - a theory that is different from existing theories - it is in our opinion the duty of the theorists to check what conditions are different from the conditions that existed when those earlier theories were formulated. In this way we always meet two questions:

- what is really new in the new theory;
- what changes in society can explain this new development in the theory.

We don't believe in mono causal explanations. The factors we mentioned until now are too complex in themselves. When talking about the *economical situation as an environmental factor*
we talk really about a large number of elements in society that have to be considered as part of the environmental factor economy.

Moreover, organization theories are influenced by the personality of the contributor and the culture of the society in which he lives. these factors will appear only marginally in the next chapters.

Conclusion

Organization theory can be seen as the result of the aspiration to generalize phenomenon in individual organizations. We have seen that organization theory has been enriched by contributions from a number of disciplines. Therefore it is important to keep a clear view on what constitutes the organization theory. In our view development in organization theory is not only a result of the advancement in the views of the contributors but as much a result of the changing conditions in the environment. This will be illustrated in the next chapters.

3. Classical Organization Theory

At the start of the twentieth century circumstances had developed so that a growing need existed for more and general principles for structuring and managing organizations. In this chapter we introduce three main characters from that period. Together they laid the foundation for what we now call organization theory. Let us begin with a look at the world of around 1900. Especially let us look at the development of the population in the countries that formed the cradle of organization theory.

Population

Abroad

Around 1870 industrial development in the United States and the most important countries of Western Europe was well under way. But in the different countries the situation was very different. One of the most remarkable phenomena was the large difference in population growth.

In table 1 we have put the population of France next to the populations of Germany, Great Britain and the United States. We see here the near stagnating population growth in France as opposed to the explosive development in the United States. The slow development in France is still more significant considering the large flow of emigrants from Germany, Great Britain and Ireland to the United States, against a negligible emigration from France.

The transition from an agricultural to an industrial society has been a complex process that changed the existing society completely. Until the end of the 18th century production of farmers was mainly directed towards their own needs and the local market. An exception was Great Britain, that, because of her colonies, already had access to a large market, especially for textiles. Textiles - especially spinning and weaving - were particularly suited for industrial production. But for the rest, however, the connections over land were so bad that they meant a real impediment to the growth of business activity. What was necessary was a revolution in traffic and transport.

	France	Gr. Britain	Germany	United States
1850	35.8	27.5		23.2
1860	36.7	29.1	36.7	31.4
1870	38.1	31.6	40.8	38.6
1880	17.0*	35.0	45.1*	50.2
1890	38.4	37.7	49.2	62.9
1900	38.9	41.5	56.0	76.0
1910	39.5	45.2	64.6	92.0
1920	39.2	44.4*	61.8*	105.7
1930	41.8	46.4	65.1	122.7
1940	41.4	47.7	70.0	131.7
1950	41.2	50.4	66.0*	150.3
*Change of territory				

Table 1: Population of a few important countries

That revolution came by introducing new methods of road building (macadam roads, after their Scottish inventor John McAdam) and especially by the development of the steam engine that could be used not only for driving textile engines but also for propelling trains and ships. The revolution in traffic and transport opened new markets so that production on a larger scale became possible and profitable.

But to supply the newly opened markets with agricultural goods a real agricultural revolution was necessary. That revolution started in the 18th century in Great Britain with the discovery that production could be improved by switching from the three-field crop rotation that was introduced in the early middle ages to a four-field crop rotation system. It then became possible to keep more cattle during winter. In the 19th century production could be dramatically improved by better irrigation techniques, the introduction of artificial fertilizers and the use of agricultural machines.

The new methods in agriculture made the farmer independent of natural fertilizers and stimulated the development of the private farm that replaced the collective agriculture of the earlier village society. Social structures were ruptured. The opening-up of new markets, however, also introduced more competition for the local producers.

The Netherlands

The development of the textile industry in the Netherlands can be used as an illustration of the processes at work. In the middle of the 19th century textile was manufactured mainly at home. Spinners and weavers did this work in part time when work in the fields was at a low level. They were free in choosing their own methods and their own hours. Their products were bought by managers and brought to the market by manufacturers. The manufacturers had in this way only little influence on the quantity they could sell and even on the moment they had the textile at their disposal.

When the import restrictions were removed in the middle of the 19th century and competition from England and Germany was felt, manufacturers had to revise their possibilities to deliver more textile of a constant quality at lower costs. Some of them had already put weavers and spinners together in one room, the factory. That gave them more grip on working hours and speed of their employees and on the quantity and quality of their products.

Making the switch to using the steam engine was no easy decision, however. To make this new technique cost-effective employees had to make more hours and show more discipline. In this new way of producing they lost much of their individual freedoms. The loss of freedom in those days was so important for the laborers that several companies couldn't find enough employees in their own region. Moreover, in the early years factory workers had to be payed more than the home workers.[17] (Luiten, 2000: 294). It seems that the most important advantage for the manufacturers was that they could eliminate the expensive managers and the production planning could be improved.

At this stage of mechanization production had to be enlarged by increasing the number of looms and the number of weavers. Therefore, not only the factory grew but the number of bosses had to increase. The growing number of weavers made it possible to specialize. New questions rose: how many bosses do we need for any given number of weavers? When the number was too large costs of production would rise unacceptably, when too small there was insufficient control on quality and

---

17 Van Zanden, 2000, 294.

production. At what point is further differentiation in labor efficient?

Elements for an Organization Theory

Distribution of Labor

As we just saw, the fast and fundamental changes in industry introduced new questions. There was a growing need for more fundamental and more general answers, for principles and guidelines. There were principles but these were brought forward occasionally without much coherence.

One of the best known principles was that of the division of labor which was as a matter of fact as old as human society itself. Even now we can find the effects of labor division in the names of streets in old cities that bear a remembrance to the handicrafts that were performed there. And yet it seems that only after Adam Smith used it entrepreneurs started implementing this principle consciously in the organization of their work. The text of Adam Smith for instance inspired the Baron of Prony, among others, who was charged with the task to create tables for logarithms and calculus. The Baron organized this work in three departments.

The first department had to develop the best method for performing the calculations. This department consisted of five or six mathematicians of a very high level. The result of their work was passed on to the second group. This second group existed of fairly good mathematicians. Their task was to transform the formulas they had gotten into simple arithmetical procedures. The third group which was the largest in number - between sixty and eighty persons - executed the procedures the second group had prepared. Of these people 90% knew only the elementary arithmetical operations of adding and subtracting.

By using this method the Baron of Prody was able to create in a few months the tables that would have cost decades to good mathematicians.[18]

Labor Cost

A major part of the discussion around organizations was about the cost of labor and the remuneration of laborers. This discussion was dominated by the contemporary opinions in political economy. According to nineteenth century political economy, the value of goods and commodities was determined by the amount of labor that was incorporated in the goods. Rewarding the labor in the production process, therefore, was an important factor in economic thought. The reward - according to Ricardo[19] - consisted on one hand of the natural price and on the other hand of the market price. The natural price of labor was the price that *'enabled the laborers to subsist and to perpetuate their race, without either increase or diminution.'* This price was different in different countries and regions and was determined mainly by the cost of food and housing and by the customs that existed in the different countries. *"An English laborer would consider his wages under their natural rate, and too scanty to support a family, if they enabled him to purchase no other food than potatoes, and to live in no better habitation than a mud cabin; yet these moderate demands of nature are often deemed sufficient in countries where 'man's life is cheap' and his wants easily satisfied."* [20]

'The market price of labor is the price that is really paid for it'. This price depends on the scarcity of labor. The market price of labor has a tendency to conform to the natural price. It is

---

18 Girard, 2000.
19 Ricardo, 1971, 115.
20 Ibidem, 118.

possible that market prices are above natural prices for a prolonged period of time. That is mainly the case in situations where an accumulation of capital goods takes place.

This opinion seems to have been common even though there were economists who had a more pessimistic view on things. They spoke of *an iron law of wages* that would keep wages unrelentingly at the minimum level of subsistence. As production was mostly performed at home or in small companies it was not unusual to pay a piece-rate. The more the laborer produced the more he got payed. But classical economists didn't expect much advancement. According to their opinion the entrepreneurs used for rewarding the laborers a fixed total sum, so if one man got more the others would get less.

Piece-rate stayed usual after the laborers were brought together in a factory for those jobs for which it was possible. Application of piece-rate in its pure form, however, meant also that laborers didn't receive anything when for any reason they couldn't work. In a number of cases a system was introduced with a warranted pay per hour and a bonus when production rose above a certain minimum.

Leadership and Authority

As long as entrepreneur and leader of the enterprise were the same person there was not much discussion about who was the boss. But at the end of the 19th century organizations and their need of capital grew. New forms of corporations emerged in which leadership and capital were separated. Ownership of the corporation rested in the hands of stockholders and leadership was put in the hands of professional managers. That lead to questions about the capabilities of managers.

Span of Control

As indicated before, the growth in the number of laborers had to lead to an increase of bosses. But how many bosses for a given number of laborers? When we start with the manager at the top then we see under him a number of supervisors or bosses who each have to supervise a number of laborers. The number of co-workers that a manager has is called his span of control. It will be clear that a large span of control will be profitable seen from the perspective of costs: the number of bosses would be small. On the other hand a few bosses would have trouble to control their workers. And as easily can be seen, a small span of control would lead to a large number of hierarchical levels what would have consequences for communication between leaders and workers. The more levels the more difficult the communication.

Great Britain

In Great Britain the use of the steam engine as an instrument of the industrial development was (in 1870) already more than a century old. As a result of the enclosure movements in the seventeenth and the eighteenth centuries large numbers of laborers had gathered in the big cities in Great Britain. In the time that was to come, they would represent the cheap labor force for the factories that emerged. The development of the industry was greatly helped by the availability of coal and iron ore in the neighborhood, but also by the dominance of Great Britain at sea, which gave good marketing possibilities in the different parts of the British Empire. Under these circumstances it was no accident that in Great Britain the first textile machines - the Spinning Jenny (1764) - came into use.

It seems obvious that in this country the start of economic theory must be sought as formulated in the works of Adam Smith, Malthus, Ricardo and Stuart Mill. It was the theory of economic liberalism that also became the most important political movement of the nineteenth century in Western Europe and the United States. It is significant that an alternative vision on labor and capital was founded in Great Britain. In 1867 in London (only a few years before the Spinning Jenny was invented) a book was published that would have a tremendous influence. In *Das Kapital* Karl Marx described what he saw as scientific socialism. His analysis , as that of Stuart Mill, was based on the theory of Ricardo and Malthus about the labor value in the price of commodities.

And Great Britain was also the country where we can find the first observations - i.e. in the writings of Babbage (1791 – 1871) - on what later would be the domain of organization theory.

United States

Immigration

Population growth in the United States in the nineteenth and early twentieth century was - when compared to the most important European countries - spectacular. Here the growth was a result of the large immigration. Estimates indicate that in the second half of the 19th century more than 40 million people entered the United States, at first mainly from Great Britain, Germany and Ireland; later the number of immigrants from Southern Europe increased. The immigrants had different motives for their coming to America. Partly they moved because of changes in Europe with a general character where industrialization created an redundancy of land labor, partly it was because of special circumstances in their own country like the famine in Ireland in the middle of the 19th century. Partly, however, they came on initiative of the American industry that during its fast expansion was in need of (skilled) laborers. The influx consisted therefore out of a very inhomogeneous mix of skilled and unskilled laborers.

There was work enough in the new home country, that in part still had to be cultivated and exploited. In the middle of the nineteenth century the fertile plains of the midwest were a near inexhaustible source for the production of wheat and meat. The biggest problem was not so much the production itself but its transport to the cities and harbors in the east where the surplus could be embarked towards the European market. Opening up the country by railway became a first priority. At the end of the civil war about 50,000 km (30,000 miles) of railways were laid. In 1890 that was 250,000 km. For the construction of these quantities of railroad large quantities of iron and steel were needed. For the production of wheels and carriages again just as much. Iron ore and coal, the most important raw materials of the industrial revolution, were available in large quantities in mines that could easily be exploited. In the northeastern part of Pennsylvania large quantities of anthracite were found. Anthracite was much harder than bituminous coal and very suited as a fuel for the production of steel. But around 1870 the production of steel was still in its infancy. It was difficult to control the process so that steel would be produced with a desired and constant content of carbon. The invention of the Bessemer converter gave the industry a decisive impetus.

A railway was built among others from the mining fields to the shipyards near Philadelphia on the Delaware. In 1866 a piece of swampy property was bought. On that land the Midvale Steel Company was built. In Midvale in 1872 an engineer, Brinley, started to improve the production of steel in a scientific way, by registering all steps and their results. He changed Midvale into one large laboratory.

Working Conditions

The development of the United States was not without risk. Many companies went broke. So the European financiers were not very keen to invest here - especially not after British speculators lost 35 million dollars in Pennsylvania.[21] The United States therefore had to rely on themselves in the period between 1850 and 1900. The necessary capital could only be raised by keeping consumption low. This was the period of the "robber barons": people like Carnegie (who took hold of the steel industry), Rockefeller (who did the same in oil) and Morgan (who controlled the railways and reformed banking). These were people without scruples, to whom laborers hardly counted. Chinese laborers were transported in closed railway carriages to the sites where they had to work on the railways. In 1889, 20,000 laborers died or got wounded during the construction of the railways[22] Strikes were mostly suppressed violently. So, for instance, was the large railway strike in 1877, that also involved the Philadelphia & Reading Railroad. This strike was brutally suppressed by the government of Pennsylvania, whereby tens of people died.

Strikes against bad working conditions were common daily occurrences. Low wages were seen as an obvious and natural phenomenon. The elite believed they had a right to their riches and believed that the poor were poor by their own doing. David J. Brewer said in 1893:

It is the unvarying law that the wealth of the community will be in the hands of the few... The great majority of men are unwilling to endure that long self-denial and saving which makes accumulations possible... and hence it always has been, and until human nature is remodeled always will be true, that

---

21 Brogan, 1985, 393.
22 Zinn, 1995, 220.

the wealth of the nation is in the hands of a few, while the many subsist upon the proceeds of their daily toil.[23]

Under these circumstances the idea of Frederick Winslow Taylor that leaders and employees of a company had a common interest and that laborers had to be thoroughly selected and trained and rewarded in accordance, was nearly totally absurd. To make this statement plausible Taylor had to show something spectacular. And that is exactly what he did. Taylor chose for that purpose one of the most simple unskilled tasks: the moving of pig iron. He showed that the production per laborer could be heightened fourfold by carefully studying the work, choosing of the right man, adjusting the equipment and systematic instruction.

Frederick Taylor

Frederick Winslow Taylor was born in 1856 in a well-to-do Quaker family. When he was 18 years old, he declined a study in law at Harvard for which he seemed to have been predestined. He took a job as an apprentice in a factory of pumps. In 1878, after four years as an apprentice, he came to work at the Midvale Steel Company. There he worked for 12 years, made a quick career and finished in his spare time his study for a degree in engineering. In Midvale Taylor developed the principles of Scientific Management.

To substantiate his ideas Taylor did not restrict himself to unskilled labor. At the time the knowledge of the processes that were applied in the factories was mainly in the hands of the laborers. And they only reluctantly passed on their knowledge to their apprentices. The owners of the factories usually didn't know exactly how the processes went nor how much time they took. The piece-rate was based on rough estimates. And if a laborer was stupid enough to deliver his work earlier than was

23 Zinn, 1995, 255.

agreed upon, his time for the next job was lowered. In that way the efficiency of the laborer was punished with wage reduction. As a worker among the workers and as a gang boss, Taylor experienced himself how laborers adopted a single course to prevent an extreme exploitation by their bosses. 'Soldiering' – using the accepted time to the fullest, even when it was not necessary – was the rule. Laborers who didn't comply were punished by their colleagues. This attitude of the laborers – that could be found in the Netherlands in the years sixty of the 20th century – was based upon a deep distrust in their employers. A distrust that was all too easily justified in their daily experience.

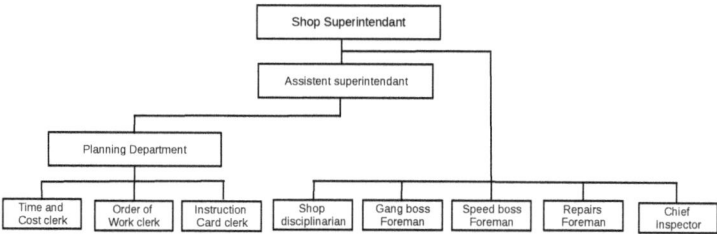

Fig.3 Functional bosses according to Taylor

Taylor had to acknowledge that with his age and experience he had insufficient knowledge to get his bench workers to use more efficient methods. He realized that he, just as Brinley had done before in the chemical processes, had to study methods in a scientific way. The first step was to ascertain an optimal speed for cutting steel on a lathe. Taylor also realized that soldiering could only be lowered if he could get a warrant for the laborers for a fair pay that would also be supported by his bosses. Here we come to the foundation of Taylors approach and conviction. Only by optimal efficiency – given an infinite market – could an organization obtain sufficient income to pay laborers according to their quality.

This is why employers and employees had a common interest in creating a high productivity. To get there it was not only necessary that laborers were educated and trained in the techniques they had to use, but the management had to accept that laborers were paid according to their knowledge and capabilities and that this pay would be guaranteed. To maintain these principles Taylor had to pursue a heavy battle as much towards the laborers as towards the management and the employers. When he left Midvale Steel in 1890 he put his ideas and his experience on paper. First in Shop Management that appeared in 1903 and later in Scientific Management in 1910.

Taylor's Ideas

In Scientific Management Taylor explained that the common interests of management and laborer best could be obtained by using the right management. The right management is founded on the following responsibilities of the managers[24]

First: They develop a science for each element of a man's work, which replaces the old rule-of-thumb method

Second: They scientifically select and then train, teach, and develop the workman, whereas in the past he chose his own work and trained himself as best he could.

Third: They heartily cooperate with the men so as to insure all of the work being done was in accordance with the principles of the science which has been developed.

Fourth: There is an almost equal division of the work and the responsibility between the management and the workmen. The management takes over all work for which they are better fitted than the workmen, while in the past almost all of the work and the greater part of the responsibility were thrown upon the workmen.

---

24 Taylor, 1913, 36.

According to Taylor, in the right management the following principles are used:

- Work has to present a continuous challenge to the worker, so that he has to make an effort to reach his goal.
- For the work standard conditions have to be created.
- Workers must be trained and instructed to apply the right working methods.
- Good performance has to be individually rewarded.
- When the agreed upon performance is not attained the award has to be lower.

To be able to apply these principles, many things in the shops have to be organized. The work process must be recorded in detail and standardized. An extensive work planning is mandatory: the workbench must be available, material, drawings and tools must be ready. The work method and the necessary time must be recorded on the instruction card. And at last: the worker must be able to check if he is on schedule. If everything is organized in this way, the necessary time must be established by time study. For the time study the work is divided into parts that are measured separately. The right time according to Taylor is not the fastest time possible but the time that belongs to a working speed that can be maintained a long time without damage to the health of the worker.

Following this line of thought the manager has to meet a number of requirements. Taylor mentions: intelligence, education, special technical knowledge or capabilities, discretion, energy, courage, honesty, judgment or common sense and a good health. There are, according to Taylor, people with three or four of these properties can be hired as a laborer. People who possess five of these properties are already hard to find. And it is hardly possible to get people with six, seven or eight of these properties. When we look with this background at the tasks and responsibilities of the chief of a workshop, we see that it is difficult to get these places filled in a reasonable way. This caused Taylor to divide the functions of the boss into jobs that can be manned by several co-workers who each can take a part of the total responsibility. Also, the selection and training of the eight bosses that are created in this way is an important point of Taylor's attention.

France

Big in Small Scale

France at the beginning of the industrial revolution had a number of problems that led to an other development. True, France possessed coal and iron ore but these were distributed in several, mostly small, fields. The coal was not of the best quality and hardly suitable to make coke – necessary for the steel production. As a result of the Napoleonic wars, France had become relatively isolated and had difficulties in finding new markets.

In this country of the revolution, where the principles freedom, equality, and fraternity couldn't be empty words, discussion on the position of the laborer was a recurring theme. In this country the principles of socialism were formulated by people like Saint Simon and Fourier and here was experimentation with forms of self-government by the laborers as in the 'familistère' of Godin in Guise.

France had hardly any proletariat that, like in Great Britain, came together in the large industrial cities.[25] This was without a doubt for a large part due to the population development, but also to the fact that the French agrarian population had (as compared to Great Britain) more owner rights on the grounds

---

25 Birnie, 1965, 28.

they explored and lived on. In France the population had to be lured into the factories by higher wages. As a result of these circumstances there was no evolution into an industry of large mass production. The small firm was dominant. In 1901 80% of the French companies had 4 employees or less.[26] But there were exceptions like the steel factories of the Schneider family in Le Creusot, were 10,000 laborers worked in 1880.

A Lack of Discipline

The war between France and Germany proved to be a bitter disappointment for France. Despite the use of a new fast repeating firearm, the French troops were defeated in a few weeks and even Paris was occupied. France had to accept the defeat reluctantly and conclude that her soldiers were of a lesser quality than those of her opponent on the other side of the Rhine. But people very soon had an explanation.

The victory of Germany was the victory of the disciplined man over he who was not. Of the respectful, well-cared for, attentive, methodical man over he who is not. Renand wrote (as cited by Girard)

This theme, a lack of discipline, was mentioned in a variety of ways by French writers from the period before World War I. Durkheim, too, refers to this theme: *The professional attitude doesn't really exist other than in a rudimentary way.*[27] Irresponsible behavior, lack of motivation, refusal to obey seem to have been normal practice.

Comparing France to Germany and Great Britain in the same period something like an explanation is forced upon us assuming that not all of it can be attributed to a difference of national

---

26 Ibid, 21
27 Durkheim, 1893, preface

cultures. In Great Britain there was already an industry for over a hundred years, where discipline could be enforced due to a superfluous supply of unskilled labor: those who did not want to obey could go away. In Germany under the leadership of Prussia during the 18th and 19th century, a military tradition had been built with the discipline that came with it.

Henri Fayol

Henri Fayol (1841- 1925) was born into a family of the petty bourgeoisie. He passed High School in Lyon and attended the mining school of Saint Etienne. He joined the coal mines of Commentry, where he would stay his whole career. When he, at the age of 25, got the responsibility of the mining concession, the company was nearly broke. Fayol succeeded in making the mines that were difficult to explore profitable. His book *Administration industrielle et générale* was published in 1916.

Fayol criticized the favoritism and nepotism that were customary in France; he criticized at the same time the low degree of discipline in business. These things were correlated he thought. He, therefore, made a plea for a more professional management of organizations and for more discipline and order. Fayol distinguished six groups of activities that have to be performed in every organization:

- Technical activities (production, manufacture, adaptation);
- Commercial activities (buying, selling, exchange);
- Financial activities (search for and optimum use of capital);
- Security activities (protect property and persons);
- Accounting activities (stocktaking, balance sheet, costs, statistics);
- Managerial activities (planning, organization, command, coordination, control).[28]

---

28 Fayol, 1949, 3.

In presenting this outline Fayol must have realized that management must be seen as a distinct task in the organization that needs separate attention.

Fayol's opinions

In the first chapter of his book, *General and Industrial Administration,* Fayol explores the possibilities of a management education. The non-existence of such an education in France, he thought, was due to the lack of a consistent theory on management. That is, he says, such a theory has not yet been presented in public. And: *without theory no teaching is possible.*[29]

As a matter of fact, according to Fayol, it is not principles which are lacking for:(...). *Who has not heard a hundred times the need for the grand principles of authority, discipline, subordination of individual interest to the common good, unity of direction, coordination of effort, foresight, etc.?* Fayol did not expect that a systematic management training would lead to only good managers, any more than that a good technical education would only deliver good engineers.

The governing of an organization comprises always the mentioned six groups of activities and therefore has a larger scope than management. *General and Industrial Administration* first examines the difference and the relative importance of these functions on different levels of the organization.

The importance that Fayol attached to management in the company can be seen in an interview in the *Chronique Sociale de France* of January 1925. On the question of what in his opinion was the best way to screen an organization and to ascertain what improvements would be necessary, Fayol replied:

---

29 Ibid, 14.

The best method is a study of what I have described as the administrative apparatus. If this is as it should be, it will be possible to secure precise information on the current situation and on the general progress of the undertaking. One can also ascertain immediately that forecasting and planning, organization, command, coordination and control are properly provided for, that is to say that the undertaking is well administered. If there are gaps in the administrative apparatus, these are often pointers to weaknesses in the organization or to faults in the running of the undertaking.

The administrative apparatus is further a concept of very wide application. Not only is it useful to those who may have to manage or control an industrial undertaking but, to my mind, its absence is a fundamental weakness in our public services and I cannot imagine a better service to our country than to ensure its application by the State. That would be the starting point for essential reforms.

What then is this administrative apparatus? It is a system of recording which includes the present, the past and the future; in which the contributions made by senior members of the staff, together with information from outside sources, ensure for the Directors the best possible means of appreciating the probable consequences of their decisions.[30]

In this way Fayol not only seems to look ahead at the decision making theories that would come up at the end of the years forty. We can read here also that the responsibility for a good functioning of the organization lies with the management, an idea that would become the center of attention in the theories around Total Management.

---

30 As cited by Urwick, 1949.

Germany

From an Agrarian to an Industrial State

The region that now is known as Germany, was, at the start of the 19th century, still a conglomerate of loose states, kingdoms and free cities. During the convention of Vienna (1815) the German Union was founded, in which 39 of these small states joined in order to create a toll-free zone. But it was not before the middle of the century that the freedom of toll was achieved. This process was strongly supported by the building of the railways.

Under influence of the French revolution and its consequences, the manorial rights of the noble were gradually abolished – first in Prussia. As a result of this the farmers who still used medieval methods to treat their land became more and more free from the bonds to their land and their lords. The same happened to the rights of the guilds, so that around 1850 the civilians in Germany were free to exercise the trade they wanted. At the end of the 18th and the first half of the 19th century, the population grew fast, which led many farmers to go to the cities. They would form the labor source necessary to start the industrialization. The slow – as compared to Great Britain and France - start of the industrial development, which didn't really take off before 1850, seems to be caused also by the low willingness to invest risk-bearing capital.[31]

The transformation of Germany from an agrarian country into a highly industrialized state was enormous. The change was supported by the formal unison after the French-German War of 1870, by the rich fields coal and iron ore and by the mentality of the German people, Tuchman states:

---

31 Walter, 1998, 78.

Goethe says at some place that if the German has to choose between unjust and disorderly he certainly will choose the first. Skilled as he is in a state where the relations between sovereign and subordinate have no other basis than obedience, he is not capable to understand a state that is founded on other principles and when he is confronted with it in reality he will feel intensely unhappy.[32]

Discipline and obedience would be for a long time characteristics of the German laborer. They were characteristics that could, under certain conditions, lead to admiration (see France). The old feudal relations did not disappear easily. And so the state held a relatively strong grip on the economic development whereby many official positions – permanent and with a good pension – emerged. The positions in the governmental organs were, until the middle of the 19th century, for about 50% occupied by higher and lower nobility. Only gradually students of the high schools and universities entered these official organizations.

This was the environment in which Max Weber wrote his observations about authority and bureaucracy.

Max Weber

Contrary to Fayol and Taylor, Weber had no experience as a manager in a company. He had been educated as an economist and belonged to the historic school of Gustav Schmoller. The historic school included many writers who saw the development of society as a natural evolution of succeeding phases. The writings of Karl Marx and especially Das Kapital also fitted in this view of a natural evolution. These writings were the subject of elaborate discussions in Weber's surroundings. Their

---

32 Tuchman, 2000, 415.

discussions were specifically focused on the meaning of the word capitalism.

These discussions in an environment with growing organizations, paternalistic relationships, and idea's about capitalism and the role of the individual made Weber focus for a long time on the phenomenon of power and leadership in relation to the legitimacy of authority.

Legitimate authority is according to Weber founded on:

- Rationality that rests on the belief of the validity of norms and rules and the right of those who, under those rules, are placed in a position to command. (legitimate authority). We find this rational authority in bureaucracy (we come back on this later).
- Tradition, the patriarchal authority has got its foundation in the family (or the tribe) where the leader has authority because he is the leader and it always has been that way. The authority is based upon the belief in the sanctity of the old traditions and the legitimacy of the status of those who exercise authority under those traditions.

Both, the rational (bureaucratic) authority and the traditional (patriarchal) authority form a stable structure of authority contrary to:

- Charisma. Charisma is not legitimated through certain structures, a particular social position or education. Charismatic authority legitimates itself by the unique properties of a certain personality. Charisma, therefore, is, by definition, a temporary kind of authority. It is part of the personality of the leader: he has authority as long as he can convince his followers.

Weber's views

Weber distinguished between the world as we see it in practice everyday and the world that could be if it was organized with 'ideal typical' constructs according to certain standards. Bureaucracy is one of those ideal typical constructs. He states that the modern bureaucratic organization is built on and functions according to a certain number of principles.[33]

1. There is or must be a certain – laid down in laws or regulations – package of tasks with matching responsibility and power to act.
    a. To form a bureaucratic organization there have to be regular activities in the form of functional duties.
    b. The necessary chain of command is given and the accompanying sanctions are limited in rules and regulations.
    c. To make it possible that functional activities are performed, it is foreseen that people are appointed with a generally accepted qualification.
2. There is a functional hierarchy that means there is a fixed system of subordination of functions. When the bureaucracy is fully implemented the functional hierarchy is monocratic. The hierarchical subordination is – at least with public functions – not the same as the competence of a person to withdraw responsibilities from a subordinate.
3. The modern functional execution of activities rests upon written texts of which the original or an copy is archived, and upon a staff of subordinate functions and writers of varying nature. The whole of activities and dossiers that belong to an official make a bureau (or an office). In modern official organizations the office is principally separated from the private accommodation.

---

33 Weber 2005, 157.

4. The function of an official – that is at least that of a specialized official – assumes an extensive training.
5. In a fully developed organization the functional activity takes all available time of all officials. Or otherwise stated: the function of an official is a full day's work (even when the workday may be limited by regulations in hours).
6. The execution of a function follows generally more or less fixed rules that can be learned. Knowledge of these rules makes up the body of knowledge of the profession the official must master and that, depending on the situation, is denoted as knowledge of commerce, of law, administration and so on.

These characteristics of the bureaucratic organization are not only found in the public services but also in the private sector: everywhere where large quantities of work have to be done or services have to be delivered and the customers or users of the services have to be served in the same way.

Historically speaking you find, Weber says, the bureaucratic organization already in ancient Egypt, but also in the Roman Empire and the Catholic Church.

The advantages of the bureaucratic organization as compared to the patriarchal form are obvious: similar cases get similar treatment and the treatment of cases is based on competence and impartiality.

Conclusion

The environmental conditions under which the theories mentioned in this chapter emerged were very different. These conditions explain the different emphasis they present. And we can see, a few points that may explain why the theory not only spread easily, but also was generally accepted.

a mentality that laid a big trust in the possibilities of technology and its possibilities.

a large, nearly unlimited market for the new products of the industrial development (machines, transport, consumer goods).

a fast growing population in most countries that provided a large supply of poor and often unskilled laborers for the new ways of production.

the absence of the old guild structures (Great Britain, United States) or their fast disappearance (France and Germany) so that the traditional production constraints fell away.

There, where these conditions existed, the views of the classical theories could be seen as actual and valid. At the same time we see that the classical theory contained a number of statements that kept their validity outside and above the actual situation and conditions.

4. Socio Technical Management

Compared to the conditions that existed in the time the classical theories were formulated, the situation after World War I was changed in many respects. On the world stage the position of the former superpowers – Great Britain, Germany and France – was weakened. Their role was taken over by the United States.

On the internal market in the United States also a lot had changed. The country had put a stop to the unlimited influx of immigrants. The car, radio and film had changed the face of society. Prosperity had risen strongly. As a result, different relations in the labor market had entered. There was reason to formulate new theory. And in view of the position of the United States at the time it was not unexpected that this was the place where new theories were born.

Technological development had been spectacular. One part of the technological change gets little attention in literature on organizations: standardization of parts, sizes and methods have made many developments in industry possible. We devote a separate paragraph to this subject.

After World War II relations in the world were even more fixed. While in the United States the enormous production capacity had come to full blossom, Great Britain – also winner of the war – was nearly broke. We will see how much different conditions influence theory when we compare the situation in the United States with that of Great Britain after World War II.

Socio Technical Management

The work of Taylor and Fayol makes up the foundation of what is called scientific management or classical organization theory. The ideas of the Scientific Management Movement were tremendously successful. Taylor's book *The Principles of Scientific Management* appeared in 1911 and was immediately translated into Chinese, Dutch, French, Lithuanian, German, Japanese, Russian, Swedish and even Esperanto. Later came a translation into Spanish.[34]

The application of Taylor's ideas influenced every sector of society. Kanigel mentions a number of books that appeared like: Household Engineering: scientific management in the home; Education and the cult of efficiency, etc. Kanigel concludes: *In the science of work, in industrial psychology, management, and machine shop practice – in all those areas, one expects Taylor to have left a deep imprint. But in so many other areas far removed from business and industry, a look back reveals that something happened early in the twentieth century to give that field its present form, and that this something was rooted in Taylor's ideas.*[35]

Apparently the work of Taylor fell in very fertile ground.

Some of the most known followers of Taylor's ideas were Frank and Lillian Gilbreth. Frank Gilbreth is best known for his work in the building business. In his observation he saw that masons in their work utilized different methods and moreover that when they worked faster they used other methods than when they worked slower. After studying their work and bettering their working conditions, he was able to improve their output from about 1000 to 2700 bricks a day. Lillian worked as a psychologist together with Frank in personnel management. After Frank died she continued his work.

---

34 Kanigel, 1997, 11.
35 Ibid., 13.

A Scientific Foundation

Taken all together it seems that in the twenties of the twentieth century organization theory had acquired a firm scientific foundation. For the theory possessed now:

- an object: the organization in all its different appearances;
- a scientific object: the efficient allocation of people and resources to realize the objects of the organization;
- a method of research.

Further development of the theory was only a matter of time or so it seemed. And indeed: everywhere and particularly in industry, analysis of work, methods and technology went on along the lines that people like Taylor and Gilbreth had spelled. Shortly after World War II and thanks to the work of Maynard, Stegemerten and Schwab, a new tool was developed: methods time measurement (MTM). MTM – in principle – made it possible to determine behind the desk the time necessary to accomplish all tasks that were done by hand.

But it appeared that there were at least two – important – problems. They were the attitude of the employers and the position taken by the unions. A large majority of the employers found the idea ridiculous that leaders and workers should work together and didn't see any reason to pay their workers according to their performance as long as they could hire workers for a lower salary. Moreover they were not very excited about the idea – as proposed by the Scientific Management Movement – that managers themselves should be qualified as leaders as this was an attack on their own position. Therefore, it is not so strange that the entrepreneurs who wanted to exploit the obvious possibilities to raise efficiency, had no real need for the advice of the consultants that concerned their own behavior. And to keep their assignments the consultants accepted the incomplete implementation of their recommendations.

The unions from their side probably had a better estimate of the power thinking of the entrepreneurs than the consultants of the Scientific Management Movement and guessed that loyalty between workers would be better served by collective wage raises than by individually directed rewarding of performance.

And so the organization-theory-to-be was attacked from two sides in the power struggle. The idea that the organization and its workers have a common interest could be thrown away as a curiosity. Or could it? Because there were dissidents like Mary Parker Follett.

Mary Parker Follett

Mary Parker Follett (1868-1933), with grades in economy, law and philosophy got the attention of businessmen through her book *Creative Experience*(1924). They were fascinated by her unusual ideas. That's why she was asked to help and solve problems in companies. Here we will occupy ourselves with her ideas on relating and solving of conflicts.

Parker Follett states that the subjective idealists overemphasize the subject and that realists do the same with the object. But subject and object are not independent entities. They influence each other. Our reality exists in the relation between object and subject. This is a dynamic relationship that is in a permanent evolution. When a subject acts the object immediately reacts and that changes the situation in which both are. As a matter of fact, this relation is even stronger: without the object, the action of the subject would be without sense. The existence of the object stimulated apparently the action of the subject. In relations you can hardly distinguish between cause and result.

The dynamic evolution of relations plays an important role in differences of opinion and conflicts. Lawyers and economists keep searching for a balance between interests and politicians keep busy looking for a power balance. But in doing so reality escapes them immediately, because a relation that was founded on a balance of power or interests evolves in time.[36]

Parker Follett therefore looks for possibilities to integrate interests. We see this in the way she handles conflicts. There are, she says, three ways to handle conflicts:

- By domination. The interest of one party prevails above the others. This may work on short notice, but almost certainly will not hold in the long run.

- By compromise. Both parties give in a little bit but no one gets what he really wants.

- By integrating the interests of both parties.

Parker Follett shows what she means in an example. A co-operative dairy factory almost went broke when the question arose as to who had to have precedence in unloading the cans at a creamery platform: the farmers that came uphill or those who came downhill. After a lot of discussion a solution could be found by making a layout so that both parties could unload at the same time.

The essence, as Parker Follett sees it, is that you shouldn't stay within the boundaries of the two alternatives that are mutually exclusive but try to get a better understanding about what the situation asks.

Not Power-Over but Power-With
Going from the integration of interests in conflict situation towards the handling of power is not a big step. Parker Follett

---

36 Graham, 1996, 35.

sees how power in society is continuously interpreted as 'power-over': power over somebody else, power over a situation. The aim of the unions of a balance of power between unions and employers (the maximum they can obtain in their negotiating position) will not lead to an optimal situation in the long run because this balance must be maintained and continuously fought for. In organizations, too, the power of a manager over his co-workers is less effective in the long run. On one hand because co-workers have the feeling they are not taken seriously and on the other hand for the managers it is possible that the power-over becomes a separate and independent part in the relationship.

For Parker Follett power and authority, and the possibility to give orders are always coupled to the situation in which they play a role. Power and authority in co-workers grow when they have room to participate. Orders will be accepted when co-workers recognize them as fitting into the situation. Power grows by managers and employees working together: it is not 'power-over' but 'power-with'.[37]

It seems clear that in the opinion of Parker Follet, management and workers must work together very closely to obtain optimum results.

Liberalism

The work of Mary Parker Follett left no deep impression in organization theory. As Drucker remarked: *...her ideas, concepts and precepts were being rejected in the 1930s and 1940s.* Time was not ripe for her views. Therefore we could call Parker Follett a dissident in relation to the mainstream of management thinking. But dissidents like Parker were not quite alone. There were also companies that stayed out of that

---

37 Ibid, 107.

mainstream. More than half a century later Peters and Waterman say: *"Right from the start", said the late Richard R. Deupree when he was chief executive officer, "William Procter and James Gamble realized that the interests of the organization and its employees were inseparable. That has never been forgotten."*[38] Procter and Gamble were founded in the middle of the 19th century.

We must realize that what was said here gives an impression of the American society. Liberalism played an important role, too, in Western-Europe as it did for instance in the Netherlands. The larger population density and the historical background - in which guilds and churches were an important factor – probably made the differences here less big than in the United States. Therefore, it is not so difficult in the Netherlands or in France to find a number of companies that proposed and implemented a social policy very early. For instance, in Delft Jacques van Marken founded the 'Gist and Spiritus fabriek' in which he practiced 'social management' with among others an organ for participation and a pension fund. Companies like Stork in Hengelo and Philips in Eindhoven or followed a similar route and took care that the housing of their employees were in accordance with the requirements of the time.

A Changed World

In the interbellum period - the period in which Parker Follett did her most important consulting – conditions for organizations in the United States had changed considerably as compared to those under which the classical pioneers had worked.

In the United States the period of the robber barons was already long ago. In the years before World War I a number of measures were taken that meant to soften up the social climate.

---

38 Waterman, 1984,76.

Between 1896 and 1917 American society underwent a critical survey of all social institutions and social practices. (Nevins, 1992: 336). This period would be called the progressive era. Not only that. In the United States – but not only there – a new middle class had emerged of doctors, lawyers and teachers; in part they had their roots in the working class, but by their education and profession were reasonably independent. They represented another and new mentality and vision towards the relation between labor and capital.

Social Change

The change in social climate was not restricted to the United States and maybe was even more obvious in Western Europe. And so in the Netherlands after the famous law against child labor from 1874, came the Labor Law from 1889, the Safety Law of 1899, the Casualties Law of 1901 and the Housing Law also from 1901.

In Great Britain a relationship was discovered between poverty and physical deprivation of the population. In 1906 measures were taken to make it possible that regular medical checks were made at schools and the serving of meals was implemented. Already since 1890 efforts were made to introduce a kind of retirement pension (starting at 70 years). A similar development took place in France.

The sharpest edges of the struggle for existence slowly eroded and for the first time in man's existence it became possible to believe in a future that would offer prosperity for everyone. Where illiteracy had been practically banned, social differences could be seen better by the working class also. And, as a result, the opinions about what was right and wrong in society and organizations would change. The poverty and suppression of the laborer was experienced as a problem that could be solved.

Economical Change

World War I changed the relative economic positions of the most important industrial countries. In France a generation of young people had been decimated, a blow that France with its traditionally low birth rate could hardly overcome. Germany was marked as loser of the war. The country was fully exhausted and had to pay heavy reparations to the allied countries. This was one of the reasons of the heavy inflation in the twenties. The chaos that resulted was a rich breeding ground for fascism in the thirties.

Great Britain had suffered huge losses, but still possessed her colonies and could still see itself as a world power. But economically it had been passed already long ago by the United States. The first World War with its long struggle in the ditches without any significant advantage for any party and its astounding number of victims, had had a stark sobering effect on the idea that war was a place to gather honor and fame.

The war had brought many victims to the United States. But war had been on foreign territory and had had another impact on the experience of the people and the productive capacity of the country had not been damaged.

Looking at the developments in the first decades of the twentieth century in the United States, one can see that in the years twenty the situation on the labor market was very different from that in years around 1880. A short characterization:

- Migration had been starkly reduced. Around 1914 the United States had put an end to the unlimited immigration. After World War I, only 150, 000 people were admitted every year. In the years before that number had been around a million.

- Government and industry agreed on the necessity to give industry a free hand (laissez faire), for industry efficiency had priority.

- The position of the laborer (and the farmer) was never seen as a problem, because economic growth was so high that in the end everybody - even the poor would gain.

- Prosperity in the United States had risen too. The per capita income of the population in 1930 was more than twice that in 1880.

- The introduction of radio, movies and cars had a strong unifying effect on values and morals.

Normalization and Standardization

Little attention in literature is payed to the fact that the efficiency of industry only could obtain its full effect by the mutual agreements – national and international – about the norms and standards that would be applied. It could be called a forgotten chapter in the history of organization theory. As a matter of fact, work in this area had already started with the introduction of the metric system on the mainland of Europe. As a consequence of the growing speed with which man could travel and with the fast improving possibilities of the means for communication, local time became a difficult to handle concept. During a meeting in Washington in 1884, therefore, agreements were made about the division of the world in time zones starting at the meridian through Greenwich (near London).

The introduction of steam engine propelled ships created the need – especially in the British Empire – to build facilities in the whole world for maintenance and repair of engines and ships. It was necessary to make agreements about sizes and qualities of appendages and spare parts.

In Europe, too, there was rising need for agreements on sizes of apparatus and parts. One of the first people who designed a worldwide standard for bolts and nuts was Joseph Whitworth. Whitworth bolts and nuts, taps and wringing irons became a household word for technicians.

In the Netherlands in 1916 the *Stichting voor de Normalisatie in Nederland* was founded. The first director of the institute was ir. Ernst Hijmans (Hijmans, 1973: 54). Hijmans had many international contacts. Thanks to the work of the numerous normalization committees many international norms were presented. Now it became possible to create chains of companies, in which some companies can be suppliers to others. Standardization and normalization had changed the face of society nearly imperceptibly, not by producing new products, but by making products compatible and portable.

After World War II standardization had become the work of the ISO, the International Organization for Standardization. ISO will not be translated into the different languages of the countries that apply the standards. In the year 2005 more than 15,000 standards had been developed, together covering more than 573,000 pages in English and French. In the ISO series of standards ISO 9000 concerns itself with requirements of management and organization.

George Mayo

George Elton Mayo, born in Australia, became known as a professor in Industrial Research at Harvard University. In that function he conducted a series of examinations in the Hawthorn Factories of the Western Electric Company in Chicago. These examinations held between 1927 and 1932 are the most extensive ever held on the attitudes and reactions of people in organizations. The examinations confirmed the idea of Mayo that for the motivation of laborers, rational and economic factors are less important than emotional and illogical attitudes and feelings. Moreover, the most important factors influencing behavior of people in organizations are those that follow from participation in groups. Therefore, Mayo said, working conditions not only need to comply with objective requirements for the work to be done, but they also and at the same time have to comply with more subjective requirements that are needed for work satisfaction. Mayo thought that people have to develop their social skills. If our technical skills lead to radical change in our working methods than we also have to develop the skills necessary to organize our lives with the results of these new working methods. (Urwick, 1956).

An elaborate report on the Hawthorne research (for the period 1927 until 1929) has been made by Roethlisberger and Dickson in *Management and the Worker*. The examinations had been preceded in 1924 by research on the relation between lighting and productivity. These examinations, however, had been inconclusive. They only left one conclusion that the research setup was not suited to find the influence of only one factor. Therefore, for the Hawthorne research project, extensive measures were taken to control all variables as well as possible. But even now the research questions had to be rephrased periodically in relation to the results obtained. The research now was aimed to determine the influence of fatigue, working conditions and the feelings of monotony on productivity.

At the Hawthorne factories worked about 29,000 employees at the time of the research. In order to make proper research possible, a separate testing space was arranged to investigate a number of variables under standard conditions. In this testing space a group of six girls composed switch circuits from parts that were available in the room. In selecting this group of six girls, the research group had started with two girls that had a –

known – good relation. These two selected the other four that should belong to the group. An additional requirement was that – to exclude learning effects from the test results – that all the members of the group should have an experience in this work of more than a year. Moreover, work was selected for which no machines were needed. In this way the group that came into being was more or less uniform with respect to background, education and experience. (Roethlisberger, 1939: 21).

In addition to the research of the work of this small group of women, interviews were held for about 1,600 workers to investigate the role of the supervisors and a similar set of interviews with the supervisors themselves. Over and above, an additional investigation was held on the social interaction in a second group of laborers. For this second group, too, a separate room was arranged.

Formal and Informal Organization

Even under these standardized conditions the research group found it difficult to draw unambiguous conclusions. Measures like changes in the payment system worked differently in the two test groups because of the interaction between the laborers and their supervisors. In their closing chapters Roethlisberger and Dickson discuss the consequences of their research for the management. They introduce the distinction between the formal and the informal organization and they state that the personnel organization is governed by systems of concepts and ideas. In the formal organization, the logic of costs and the logic of efficiency are dominant; in the informal organization, the logic of feeling influences the behavior of the employees. The logic of feeling represents the values of human relations of the different groups in an organization.

The logic of feeling may be compared to the concept of organizational culture that emerged after World War II.

According to Roethlisberger and Dickson the role of management is twofold:

- To ensure that the goals of the organization are reached.

- To maintain the balance in the internal organization in a way that the individual workers - by contributing to the common goals - experience a personal satisfaction that makes them willing to cooperate.

In the personnel organization, management is confronted with three important questions:

- Problems that are connected to changes in the social structure.
- Problems of control and communication.
- Problems connected to the fitting in of individuals in the social structure.

Both C.G. Stoll, in the preface, and Mayo, in his introduction to the book of Roethlisberger and Dickson, state that the results of the research could only be reached thanks to the open-hearted cooperation between researchers and workers (Roethlisberger, 1939: viii/xiii). This statement of course can be seen as a confirmation of the opinion of Taylor that maximum productivity can only be reached when managers and workers work together heartily.

The book of Roethlisberger and Dickson did not appear before 1938.

World War II and After

Most of the allied winners of the Second World War were not in good shape. The countries that had been occupied were confronted with big losses in their productive capacity. It is true that Great Britain had not suffered from an occupation but it had other reasons for a position that was not at all enviable (see par 4.5.1). On the other hand the big losers – Germany and Japan – were nearly broke as a result of the heavy bombardments in the later years of the war. They only could rebuild a new position thanks to financial help of the United States.

The United States had directed its industry completely towards war production and thereby had build a productive capacity without parallel. This capacity could partly be re-allocated for civil consumption. But because of the threat that emanated from the Soviet Union this time the army was not dismantled in a big way. On the contrary, the growing contrast between the western countries and the Soviet Union led to the Cold War and the related arms race. The United States would allocate a permanently high part of its budget to war expenses.

The United States

Tensions on the Labor Market

In spite of the war, the situation on the labor market was one of tension. The years 1944 till 1947 knew many strikes. The most annoying part for the laborers was that the enormous profits that business made during the war only meant limited wage increases. But the situation was not very much in favor of the unions. The right to strike from the Wagner Act had been a thorn in the flesh of the conservative forces. Now after the War they succeeded against the will and even the veto of the democratic president Truman to get the Taft-Hartley Act approved. That act nullified most of the Wagner Act.

How sharp relations were at the time can be illustrated by the remark of Peter Drucker.

To give an example: In the 1940s, Charles E. Wilson, the recently appointed CEO of General Motors (GM), wanted to introduce what we now call 'quality circles' and a partnership between management and workers based on workers' responsibility for their own work and tasks – practices we now credit the Japanese with. To find out what questions workers considered important, Wilson ran a company wide survey. The workers' response was overwhelming. But before GM could take any action, the United Auto Workers (UAW) protested to the National Labor Relations Board that even asking workers about their jobs was an 'unfair labor practice'. And it threatened to pull the GM laborers out on strike. The survey implied the possibility of cooperation between company and workers, that there were areas in which both had the same interests – in other words, that there could be harmony. According to UAW this violated the axiom of conflict on which both the country's labor law and the union contracts were based.

I knew one of the NLRB members and went to Washington to talk to him about the issue. He was a Republican appointee and under daily attack from the union as 'pro-management'. But when I said something about management and workers having "a common interest in the survival and prosperity of the company" (...) my friend cut me short: "Any company that asserts such a common interest", he said, "is prima facie in violation of the law and guilty of a grossly unfair labor practice." He continued: "Labor relations have to be war; and their end cannot be "harmony"; it must be victory for one side and defeat for the other. The best you can hope for are rules of civilized warfare and armistice long enough for each side to bury its dead."[39]

---

39 Drucker, 1996, 5.

Changing Consumer Market

This all may not have been so bad for the position of the laborer in a growing economy. And economy boomed thanks to the fact that international competition had disappeared, an enormous external market and high spendings on defense. And yet in the years fifty and sixty the consumer market showed signs of saturation. Packard showed in *The hidden Persuaders*[40] how the American industry used subtle ways of advertising to stimulate higher household spendings. And in *The Waste Makers* [41] he showed that industry artificially shortened the life cycle of consumer goods to keep production rising (or in terms of our time: planned obsolescence.)

One of the most obvious examples of shortening the life cycle of products was in the car production. Consumers were with ever more emphasis talked into believing that cars were out of date after one or two years and did not comply to the latest trend. And in the years fifty there were very little innovative products. The profit making models of the period had all been introduced in the years before the war.

American society of that period – the years between 1945 and 1960 – can be characterized as a static society without foreign competition. There is reason to assume that the requirements for management functions in business were not very high. Business schools may indeed have been a proper education for management in business. It is in this period of relatively low innovation that there was room for the development of the ideas that emerged out of the Hawthorne-research in the so-called Human Relations Movement. This movement was most popular in the years between 1945 and 1960, but many ideas of people like Kurt Lewin, Rensis Likert, Chris Argyris and Fred Herzberg

40 Packard, 1963, 1.
41 Packard2, 1963, 2

would find their way into the later theories of organization development. Part of the new theories was directed towards the motivation of people in organizations. Among those theories the views on the need-hierarchy of Maslow (1908 - 1970) who emphasized the fact that higher needs will become actual to the extent that lower needs are satisfied.

Great Britain

Large Debts

It is true that Great Britain emerged victorious out of the war but the country was nearly broke and had fallen into poverty. The burden of debt was enormous. The supply of war material could only be financed on the ground of the Lend-Lease Act that had been approved during the war. This act made it possible that Great Britain could buy material for warfare with the condition that the bill would not have to be paid until after the war. So immediately after the war the British government was confronted with a debt to pay for which no means were available. Moreover, the government had given promissory notes as compensation for the contributions of the countries of the commonwealth which caused an additional debt to the countries of the sterling area.

To confront the difficulties the British government had to pursue a policy of soberness for a considerable period thereby stimulating the export at the cost of internal consumption.

Already during the war a remarkable shift towards the political left took place in Great Britain. This resulted in the fall of the Churchill government directly after Germany surrendered. A labor government was formed under Attlee. The cabinet Attlee undertook a strong socialist policy by nationalizing large parts of the industry, implementing free health care, raising salaries and pensions and implementing a child allowance. In this case the new government worked close together with the unions (who had their former chairman Bevin in the cabinet). The most important issues for the unions were better working conditions and better consultation institutions.

Brown and Jaques

Wilfred Brown was already CEO of the Glacier Metal Co from 1939 onwards. In this position he was determined to apply scientific methods and knowledge to every aspect of management. Therefore, he worked together with Elliott Jaques in the Glacier Project for sixteen years. The results of their cooperation were put in a number of books written by Brown as well as by Jaques. Important views of Brown are:

-It is necessary to use a good defined language to be able to talk and communicate about organizations and their design. Brown uses the concept of 'boundary defined concepts'.[42]
-There must be a balance between the work to be done, the capabilities of the people who do it and the reward they receive.
-In analyzing the relations between managers on one hand and specialists and other workers on the other, Brown distinguishes staff-authority, the power to give instructions to co-workers when these instruction are within his field of competence and within the established policy of the manager.[43] This approach means that Brown breaks with the concept of unity of command.

Brown pays much attention to the representative system. This subject, together with the related subjects of power in the organization, policy making, methods of appeal and wage

---

42 Brown, 1971, 9.
43 Idem, 109.

differences, takes about 25% of the contents of his book and shows the importance in the eyes of Brown. The representative system makes it possible to review differences of opinion between managers and their co-workers at the highest level in the organization but, in the opinion of Brown, is separated from the executive system.

The discussion on wage differences is built on research and work of Jaques who emphasizes the importance of:

- the timespan of discretion. In this concept Jaques introduces a relation between the level of the work done and the time that expires before a decision of a co-worker can be judged. The longer the timespan the higher the level of the work. On the basis of the timespan, Jaques distinguishes five levels of work.
- the relation between age and capacity of co-workers. As a result of his research on data on careers of companies in Great Britain and in foreign countries, Jaques was able to draw growth curves that allowed him to make predictions about potential possibilities for employees.

The analytical work of Brown and Jaques' research made it possible to lay a rational basis under the negotiations between management and workers in the company and with the unions to prevent unnecessary conflicts on labor conditions and wages. In that way we can see that the views of Brown were a direct answer to the difficult situation on the labor market in Great Britain in the period after the second World War. After 1971 the views of Brown slowly disappeared. But then conditions on the British labor market had changed considerably.

Conclusion

The American economy in the period between 1920 – 1960 experienced little or no competition from other countries and showed a continuous growth. This gave a stable basis for business that showed little innovation in the second half of this period.

Prosperity of the population rose very fast. The primary needs of the labor population seemed to be satisfied. According to Maslow it now was time for less materialistic needs. Theories on human relations and motivation gave these views a theoretical background. In Great Britain however – under the pressure of the economical situation after the second World War and the existing relations – a theory was formulated (Wilfred Brown) that fitted these relations perfectly. That these views flourished only a short time shows that in Great Britain conditions changed very fast over time.

5. Contingency Management

The period of the socio-technical management started in our view around 1940 and we let it end around 1960. It was a period in which American business had nearly no competition from abroad. Partly this was caused by the isolationist policy of the United States between the two World Wars, but it was strongly influenced, of course, by the effects of the war that had nearly destroyed the former competitors. Around 1960 this situation came to an end. The new conditions called for new theories.

In the nextparagraph we shall see how the United States faced the new challenges. In the long run, however, the new views were insufficient. We will see that around 1980 conditions had changed again so that new views were necessary.

In the paragraph thereafter we will look at the developments in the Netherlands under different conditions as a contrasting case.

United States

The books of Vance Packard (see page 37) were very popular. They demonstrated the enormous success of the American way of production and at the same time the growing concern about the unlimited mountains of waste that emerged. To keep factories running, factories would have to be built in such a way that the assembly lines could be directed – according to the demand – towards the market of dealers and consumers or towards the back of the factory on the top of a hill where products could be thrown away. Not everybody seemed to be enthusiastic about that prospect. And moreover a production system in which products had a declining life cycle led to a production with a declining quality standard. Johnson says:

'By the 1950s, American cars had become technologically out of date, impractical and unsafe cathedrals of chrome, manufactured sloppily and sold using methods that can only be described as shameful. The Buick and Oldsmobile of 1958 were huge, vulgar, dripping with pot metal and barely able to stagger down the highway. (...) As a result the Japanese car industry was able to do to GM what GM had done to Ford in the 1920s.'[44]

In 1960 the world outside the United States had already changed. The economies of Western Europe but particularly those of Germany and Japan had fully recovered from the war damages. Compact cars from Germany had become a synonym for reliability and safety. For the first time in many years the American industry had to face competition from abroad.

But it was not only competition that changed. In the middle of the 1950s the first computers – mainly designed for military purposes in the second world war – came available for business purposes. They signaled the start of a whole new world of products and professions and new ways of production.

There were more changes. The anti-communist campaigns had lost its most sharp edges but the fear of communism led the United States towards the war in Vietnam. That war would grow till it became one of the most frustrating questions the United States had ever known.

Internally the black population of the United States demanded attention for their backward position. Race riots caught the attention everywhere in the country. The battle was heavy and bitter and reached a historic low in the murder of Martin Luther King in 1968.

---

44 Johnson, 1999, 731.

In the years sixty a new generation of Americans came to adulthood that had not known the second World War. They – the baby boomers as much in Europe as in the States – gave society a new energy and optimistic view on the world.

The relative stability of the fifties was over. There was indeed a new dynamic situation. There was reason for new contributions to organization theory. We will here take a look at the work of Lawrence and Lorsch and the work of Ansoff.

Lawrence and Lorsch

In 1967 Lawrence and Lorsch investigated the possible relation between different sets of technical and economical constraints and the patterns of organization and control that would lead to successful businesses.

Starting point of their investigation was the idea that an organization can be seen as an open system in which the behavior of individual members of the organization are interrelated. To understand the behavior of managers in larger organizations, Lawrence and Lorsch concentrate on the different patterns of differentiation and integration that are applied in organizations. In their study they see differentiation as: *the difference in cognitive and emotional orientation among managers in different functional departments.*[45]

Apparently Lawrence and Lorsch were not directly interested in the actual allocation of activities over departments, but in the phenomenon that people of a discipline as a group create their own culture. (This phenomenon had already been observed by Hijmans in his theory on organizational climate.) To compensate for differentiation, forms of integration are necessary. Lawrence and Lorsch do not see integration as an

---

45 Lawrence, 1967, 11

activity that leads to working together, but in their own words *the quality of the state of collaboration that exists among departments that are required to achieve unity of effort by the demands of the environment.*

In the environment Lawrence and Lorsch distinguish:

- the technical and economical security.
- the uncertainty of the market.
- the certainty of the relevant scientific developments.

To achieve integration conflicts between departments must be resolved. Lawrence and Lorsch distinguish three ways to handle conflicts: Confrontation (problem-solving), smoothing-over and forcing. We see here an approach that resembles that of Parker Follett.

In general we find the integrative role in an organization allotted to a department of integrators. The efficiency of the organization is related to the orientation of the integrators.

Lawrence and Lorsch do not give a general theory on organization. They point to the need of organizations to adapt their mechanisms for differentiation and integration to the dynamics of their environment. They conclude that successful organizations adapt better than less successful organizations.[46] Which does not surprise us very much.

Ansoff

Growing competition from, among others, Japan, meant that the market in the United States was not unlimited. It became necessary to tune production of the firm to the possibilities of the market. Therefore, a growing number of companies started to

---

46 Ibidem, 11.

use analytical methods to come to grips with strategic decisions.[47]

Ansoff was aware of the relation between the results of an enterprise and the decisions taken inside the organization. These decisions, he says, can be divided into three groups:

- Operating decisions, that is decisions that are directed towards daily routine in the organization. Under these decisions also the decisions to allocate means to functional and production departments, check performance, etc.
- Administrative decisions; that are those decisions that are meant to keep resources of the company in optimal condition. These comprise decisions that influence the organization structure, authority and hierarchy, workflow control, attract and develop resources, selection and appointment of personnel, personnel development etc.
- Strategic decisions. These decisions relate primarily to the relation between the organization and its environment. That means it is about questions like: what kind of an enterprise do we want to be, what markets do we want to penetrate, do we have to specialize or not and, if so, how far?

In *Corporate Strategy* Ansoff concentrates on the strategic decisions. And because strategic decisions have a long time bearing on the position of the company, Ansoff really looks at the long time perspectives of the company. His goal is to create a format that allows for a systematic approach of strategic decisions. Strategy has a long term orientation and that means that the decisions have to consider the uncertainties inherent to the long term. The farther the company tries to look ahead the more uncertain the prognostics and the forecasts. Ansoff is

---

47 Ansoff, 1965, 21.

aware of these uncertainties and sees at the same time that strategy is different for every company because every company is different and its market position differs from that of other companies.

The strategic discussion doesn't stand alone; it influences and is influenced by other discussions in the organization. The strategy discussion feels the pressure of the daily operational decisions and at the same time the strategic discussion has to meet the constraints of the limited means of the organization; the allocation of resources for strategic purposes prevents those means being spent on other possibilities.

In the view of Ansoff, strategic decisions shouldn't be taken as such; but they should have an underlying common characteristic before they are taken into account. As a matter of fact, Ansoff himself found it difficult to discover such a common characteristic.

Product Market	Today	Future
Present	Market share	Product development
New	Market development	Diversification

Table 2 The Ansoff matrix

Therefore Ansoff presents a simple model to explain the ideas behind the strategy discussion. (See table 2).

Ansoff presents in his matrix the following components:

- The existing product-market combination in which the company works

- The growth vector that shows in which direction the company develops. In the matrix this development is represented as the development of the market share.
- The competitive advantage, that shows in which fields the company has a strong position compared to its competitors.

These components can be seen as as many common characteristics that have to be considered as part of the strategy discussion. Ansoff distinguishes another, a fourth component: the synergy that emerges from a certain strategy from using the strong points of the company.

Organization development

As according to Lawrence and Lorsch different environments ask for different organizations and if according to Ansoff different strategies might lead to different organizations, organizational change could be expected. But how do you do that? In the years 1960 a new school of management consultants emerged that concentrated on the processes of change. At first change was supposed to be a change from one stable state to another. This was done as Kurt Lewin thought: unfreeze your organization – adapt to the new environmental requirements and freeze it. It didn't take long to realize that organizational change had to be a continuous proces. The new way of thinking was organizational development.

Organization development is an answer to change. It is a complex educational strategie that is directed towards a change in beliefs, in opinions, attitudes, values and structures that exist in an organization so that the organization can adapt to new technologies, markets and other challenges and even to the extraordinary speed of changes themselves.[48]

---

48 Bennis, 1974.

The Netherlands

In the first years after 1945 all energy in the Netherlands was directed towards overcoming the damage caused by the war. In that period there was a shortage of practically everything, so that, for every practical purpose, market conditions were favorable. As a matter of fact the conditions in the Netherlands just after the war were in many ways not unlike the conditions in the United States around the beginning of the 20th century. In this period Scientific Management proved again to be very useful. In the industry systems of performance measuring and rewarding – modified piece rate systems - were implemented in a big way.

At the beginning of the 1960s these systems gradually lost their attractiveness. The employees started to make objections and employers gradually changed to systems of group rewarding and merit rating.

One aspect of the rebuilding of industry was that much was invested in the process industries. Around 1950 the value of assets in process industries were 77% of total industrial assets (of the 100 most important companies). Luiten van Zanden[49]

Generally speaking the strength of the Netherlands seems to be in process industry.

The relationship between employers and employees in the Netherlands differed greatly with that in the United States. According to Luiten van Zanden[50] The famous 'conducted wage policy' that was introduced in 1945, was in many ways a continuation of the system of collective wage bargaining that existed during the interbellum. Just as important was the experience during the German occupation, that created a

---

49 Van Zanden, 1997, 62
50 Van Zanden, 1997, 111.

psychological climate for the institutionalized cooperation after the war. The most concrete example was the founding of the *Stichting van de Arbeid,* (Labor Foundation) as a result of secret negotiations between representatives of the three most important labor unions and the employers association during the war.

As a matter of fact the *Stichting van de Arbeid* proved to be a key factor in the social-economic governing of the Netherlands. The model of consultation that laid at the bottom of the governing was of course scrutinized intensively. The representatives of the different levels were followed suspiciously and for them a good communication with their supporters was essential for their possibilities to succeed. It is plausible that this societal background explains why the problems of governing got a relatively important interest particularly in the Netherlands.

A Governing Paradigm

So it is not accidental that interest in the Netherlands after World War II concentrated on the governing of processes and governing of the organization as a whole. Representatives of this opinion are Kampfraath, De Leeuw and In 't Veld. They see the governing of organizations as a separate phenomenon, that has its own requirements. When we look at the processes of governing in organizations, we can distinguish between a governing organ and a governed organ. According to De Leeuw, the governing organ is not a separate unit in the organization that can be studied separately. The governing of the organization takes place throughout the whole organization. Thereby the emphasis can be placed differently. De Leeuw assumes that a model of the governed organ is required in order to be able to analyze the process of governing. Kampfraath, whose approach will be called the Wageningen approach, presumes that the governing processes can be analyzed apart from the properties of the governed organ. The governing process, he says, has a number of characteristics that will be found in any situation. The governing process consists of a number of decision processes that can be divided in two fields of attention: on one hand the care for the availability of capacity (also called creation of capacity) and on the other hand the care for the use of the capacity.

Inside the field of capacity creation there are always two governing tasks:

- governing capacity that leads to a tuning of means and ends and has to answer the question: what capacity do we need – expressed in resources, qualities and number of employees? These are decisions that have long term consequences, therefore the results have strategic implications. (the strategic task)
- the conditioning task directed towards the governing of the available resources. This task is about the care that the resources, necessary for the execution of sales or production plan, are available in the required quality and quantity. In this task we see the evaluation of alternatives and making the right choices in obtaining resources, appointing and educating people. Also, the choices around remuneration and other aspects of personnel management belong to this task.

Kampfraath distinguishes also two governing tasks in the field of the use of capacity.

- The realization task. This task ensures that the available resources will contribute to the governed processes in the right way. This task has to answer the question of who does what and with what resources. This task is oriented towards the production techniques.

- The operational task is comprised of choices about the logistics of the production process and gives answers to the question of what must be reached at what time.

This division gives a framework in which every situation that occurs can be placed. By working out this framework for every situation, the individual situation is always analyzed in relation to the whole.

Using the distinction in governing tasks as a starting point gives the possibility to evaluate the way these tasks are executed. The quality of the decision making can then be tuned to the requirements of the process in that organization so that custom-made solutions to organizational problems can be offered.

Moreover, by abstracting from the actual occupation of positions, the Wageningen approach proves to be applicable to analyze organizational problems in different cultures and make them negotiable. A specific application of the Wageningen approach can be found in the integrated flow of material. Here the (theoretical) discussion is extended above the level of the individual organization. Starting with the management of agrarian chains, this discussion has gradually expanded to the general problem of chain management.

A Wave of Democratization

In the years sixty of the 20th century, the stress of the years before, resulting from the the crisis in the thirties and following World War II, seemed to be released and turned into a general opposition against authority. For many people this opposition had its roots in their dissatisfaction with the existing social structures. It was a movement that was not restricted to the Netherlands but was here very outspoken. The resistance against existing structures was so prevalent that even the leading elite became convinced of the necessity of social change.

Business absorbed new ideas from the United States about task enrichment and task structuring based on the ideas of, among others, Kurt Lewin. These ideas got the wind behind them because of – as Zwart put it – two developments.

- The extension of compulsory education, that resulted in smaller numbers of employees with only primary education.
- The attractiveness of the services sector that proved to be able to offer appealing jobs to particularly youthful female personnel.

At the end of the fifties business was confronted for the first time with the consequences of a fast growing prosperity and a situation of almost permanent full employment: a much more critical attitude towards the work offered, at first with the newcomers on the labor market and later also with the elder employees.[51]

Organization Development

In organization theory we see the spirit of the sixties in the views on organization development. The model of organization development of the NPI (Nederlands Pedagogisch Instituut), which was very popular in the Netherlands, presented a nearly equal position of managers and workers in implementing changes in organizations. We find this model also in the just mentioned book of Zwart.

The model of the NPI moves between two polarities:

- The tension between past and future.
- The tension between concepts and reality.

The model comprises five phases:[52]

---

51 Zwart, 1973, 85.
52 Glasl, 1975, 8.

- Orientation.
- Exploration of existing situation and future.
- Operational goals and operational analyses.
- Experimental projects and experimental situations.
- Realization.

Though the basic assumption seems to be that the initiative for organization development lies at the top of the organization, Glasl & De la Houssaye don't pay much attention to the role of the management of the organization. The most they say about it is that the top most of the time decides on goals of and policy in the organization.

From this period several models of organization development emerged. They had as a common characteristic that they all assumed a change throughout the whole organization.

Management and Culture

Change in the American Economy

As we saw before, the quality of American cars had become rather poor in the 1960s so that it created a market for Japanese cars. It was not only in the car industry that competition was felt. Around about 1960 the Japanese cameras became known. They competed with the German brands – famous for their quality – for first place in their field. In this period the American industry put priority on quantity to accommodate the worldwide demand for products and neglected more or less the care for quality.

Around 1980 there were problems apart from the growing competition that forced American business to change. Reagan had taken over the White House from Jimmy Carter who had left a poor heritage: high inflation, large unemployment and a large budget deficit that seemed to have become permanent. Oil prices had exploded and in general Carter had not had a lucky hand in foreign affairs.[53] Carter had not been able to take away the feelings of frustration after Vietnam and Watergate. The American confidence had been badly damaged and had not yet fully recovered when Reagan took over.

Popularity of Reagan was remarkably high and stayed high even though he was not always very strong with regard to the contents of his policy. His big merit in the eyes of the American people was that he had only a simple message and could communicate it very well; he was the Great Communicator. Reagan thought that for the situation America was in, government was not the solution, government was the problem. In this regard Reagan got strong support from the Chicago school of Economics lead by Milton Friedman.

Because he felt that individual initiative would boost the economy, Reagan worked for lower taxes, less red tape and a stronger position of the individual states. With the support of Congress, Reagan succeeded to implement in a short time an important part of his plans. Both parties in Congress shared the opinion that something had to happen to boost the economy even without knowing what that something had to be.

What Reagan did in politics found its counterpart in the work of Peters and Waterman.

Peters and Waterman

The book of Peters and Waterman, *In search of Excellence*, became an international bestseller. It took up the feeling that the efficiency of American management was no longer perfect and surely not good enough to take up the challenge from Japan.

---

53 Nevins, 1992, 618.

Luckily there were American companies that were functioning alright. In their research, Peters and Waterman tried to find out how successful companies differed from less successful ones. In their analysis they explored the rational organization model and the motivation of the working man before setting out their new theory.

In the chapter on motivation Peters and Waterman get rid of the idea of the rational deciding man. According to them, excellent companies know that their employees are just a sample of society, so the quality of their employees will be average. By correlating the goals for the employees to this average, these companies succeed in giving their employees the feeling of being successful and having an important contribution to the results of the company.

In the third chapter – Back to the Basics – Peters and Waterman emphasize the importance of organization culture. According to them, the excellent companies succeed in creating a positive culture by emphasizing only a few goals, a simple organization and a limited (lean) staff. On their way to formulating a new theory Peters and Waterman present eight basic principles that – according to them – are used by the best managed American companies.[54]

- *One. A bias for action: a preference for doing something – anything – rather than sending a question through cycles and cycles of analyses and committee reports.*
- *Two. Staying close to the customer – learning his preferences and catering to them.*
- *Three. Autonomy and entrepreneurship – breaking the corporation into small companies and encouraging them to think independently and competitively.*

---

54 Waterman, 1984, coverpage.

- *Four. Productivity through people – creating in all employees the awareness that their best efforts are essential and that they will share in the rewards of the company's success.*
- *Five. Hands on, value driven – insisting that executives keep in touch with the firm's essential business.*
- *Six. Stick to the knitting – remaining with the business the company knows best.*
- *Seven. Simple form, lean staff – few administrative layers, few people at the upper levels.*
- *Eight. Simultaneous loose-tight properties – fostering a climate where there is dedication to the central values of the company combined with tolerance for all employees who accept those values.*

Looking at these eight basic principles they seem to be a nearly literal translation of the political program of Ronald Reagan but then concentrated on the individual company. The importance of the desired organizational culture mirrors perfectly the culture of society as stimulated by the government. The book was, as Naisbitt put it, *perfectly timed.* (Naisbitt on the cover of *In Search of Excellence*).

In *In Search of Excellence* Peters and Waterman present also the very well known 7S-model of consulting agency McKinsey, where both authors had worked. It was not the first book to put emphasis on the importance of organization culture, but it became a bestseller in the whole Western World as a result of its perfect timing. And it was followed by a stream of books on organization culture.

Broadening the Scope

The discussion around *In Search of Excellence* also shows that the American industry after 1980 could no longer ignore the growing economies elsewhere. In the first place, of course, was Japan. The spectacular performance of Japanese industry led to the question of how Japanese businesses had been able to become a world- leading economy. After scrutinizing the situation, it proved that at the foundation of the Japanese success was a system that was not really new and not even really Japanese.

In the 1920s Shewhart introduced at the Bell Company the quality control card. This card made it possible to distinguish between accidental errors and systematic errors in industrial processes. It now became possible to produce products with equal and constant quality. The observations of Shewhart and his pupil Demming were detailed in a system of statistical quality control and were used in, among other things, the American war industry. It was one of the factors that made the the enormous American production in the war possible.[55]

When the American army – after the Japanese surrender in 1945 - took over Japan, the communications infrastructure and apparatus proved to be of a very uneven and fairly low quality. Under those circumstances, it was plausible that Deming (one of the American experts) was asked to give a number of lectures on statistical quality control and the way that it could be implemented in an organization. The Japanese management absorbed the system completely and by doing so demonstrated the possibilities of cooperation between management and workers. The system, as elaborated in Japan, came to be known under the name Total Quality Control and was written down by Kaoru Ishikawa (1985).

There is reason to believe that the Japanese culture (more collectivistic) was better suited for extensive application of Total Quality Control than the American culture, that is more

---

55 Ishikawa, 1985, 14.

individualistic and where the opposition between management and workers is much bigger.[56]

But it is also clear that organization theory after 1980 was no longer an exclusive American question. It became more and more the result of international influences and contributions.

Conclusion

The period since 1945 is the longest period in modern history without armed conflict between the most technically and economically developed countries. It is a period in which the countries of Western Europe and Japan developed enormously. After 1960 this became noticeable in the slowly changing competitive position of the United States. In this period we see new views in organization theory emerge on planning and strategy and on the relation between structuring the organization and its environment.

On the other side we see that another environment (i.e. the Dutch) leads to other developments. More generally, we can see that growing international competition leads to a more complex environment for organizations and to a theory that incorporates more factors and aspects. More and more, the organization is seen as an integrated whole. Attention is no longer focused on the proper organization, but also on the strengths and weaknesses of competitors (organization culture) and on the mutual relations between organizations (networks and chain management).

---

56 Hofstede, 1994, 79.

6. A Few Theoretical Notions

In this chapter we will examine a few technical aspects of organization theory that influence its development. Though they are mentioned casually in the previous chapters they get hardly any attention in literature.

The Scientific Object

In chapter 1, we defined the scientific object of organization theory as the most efficient allocation of people and means to

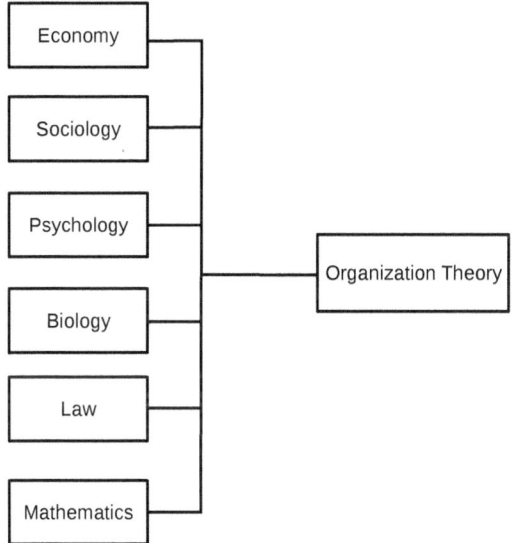

Fig. 4 Disciplines with an important contribution
to organization theory

reach the goals of the organization. This scientific object of the theory can be easily recognized in classical organization theory.

The most efficient allocation of people and means is the result of decisions about that allocation. Therefore one shouldn't be surprised that decision making has become one of the major issues in the course of the history of organization theory.

Organization theory is not the product of only one discipline. Already Taylor made use of mathematics to support his research. We saw also that Frank Gilbreth worked closely together with his wife, the psychologist Lillian Gilbreth, to enlarge the knowledge of the behavior of people in organizations. Psychology was used in the first place in the selection of workers. In the course of history, several other disciplines have contributed to organization theory. We mention, for instance, new sciences such as systems theory, cybernetics and also economy and sociology. See also fig 4.

Probably the most important of the contributing disciplines are (organization) psychology and (organization) sociology. These are disciplines that have their own scientific object and therefore their own vision on the questions they examine. For instance, March and Simon state: *Seen from the position of the social psychology we are interested in the way the individual is influenced by its environment and how he reacts on these influences.*[57] Their scientific object is clearly that of social psychology.

We agree with the writers when they say that knowledge of this object is very important to the manager. But to the organization theory not every influence by the environment on the individual is relevant. Especially reactions of the individual that occur under circumstances that are applicable in organizations are important. That is, an environment in which power relations are expressed permanently. But moreover the manager and the organization theory have to take into account the reaction of the

---

57 March, 1969, 2.

individual to the necessity to realize the goals of the organization. The statements of March and Simon have to be understood against that background.

Validity and Actuality of Theories

The theories we examined in the chapters 3, 4 and 5 were not chosen at random; they mark important changes in the opinions about organizations and about the management of organizations. They are chosen also because they cover a large part of the history of the organization theory. And we have chosen theories that have survived over time: we find them in practically every textbook. One could say these theories were at once valid and actual.

We see a theory as valid when the relation between variables, as given by the theory, can be demonstrated under the circumstances that are indicated in the theory. The theory, for instance, that water boils at 100° Centigrade and a pressure of 1 atmosphere can be seen as a valid theory.

A theory is actual if the theory is valid and the circumstances under which the theory is valid correspond to those under which the theory is valid. The statement that water boils at 100° Centigrade and a pressure of 1 atmosphere is still valid at high altitude but it is no longer actual.

When we look at the organization theory we see hardly any attention to the conditions under which the theory is valid. Undoubtedly, this is partly caused by the character of the organization theory. This is very much directed towards applicability in practice, more than it is towards actuality.

When we say this, it is remarkable that the theories of Taylor and Fayol, that were founded respectively in metal construction and mining, could be applied to practically every sector of human activity. Apparently Taylor and Fayol had formulated a number of principles with – at that moment – a very broad validity and high actuality. They were applied in small and large organizations, in organizations in different industries and in different cultures.

The fact, however, that new contributions to the theory are accepted as generally valid does not mean that they will be relevant (actual) for all organizations to the same degree. A single example may make this clear.

The rule that a manager should have only a limited span of control because otherwise the quality of his leadership will decrease, is only significant for those organizations that have a large number of employees. How valid the rule is otherwise is hardly important for the large number of organizations that have five employees or less.

A similar observation can be made with regard to the dynamics of the environment. We can easily accept that the dynamics in the environment of a bakery has increased in the last fifty years when we only look at the product assortment the baker is supposed to sell. Yet this growing dynamics will seldom lead to the use of new and separate mechanisms of integration. The size of the organization also makes that theory, in this case, is not actual despite the fact that the environment is clearly important.

Size of an organization is apparently significant for the actuality of a number of principles of the theory and dynamics of the environment is clearly one of the principles that is affected.

If the size of the organization is largely decisive for the problems of control in an organization, then it is possible to conclude that the principles of the organization theory are actual in the first place for those organizations in which the problem of control has reached a certain level. We must also consider that the problems of control is unevenly spread over the different activities of management. So we see that for an Internet company that has a limited number of customers but a large number of suppliers, the control problems emerge from the large number of goods he has to deliver. On the other hand, we see the newspaper, that has only one product, that has to be distributed over a large number of places and clients. This company has to make sure that there is sufficient personnel for distribution. So it is always the person, who has to solve a problem, who has to decide whether a theory is valid and actual in his case.

Private Theories

We have already characterized organization theory as a body of knowledge, a collection of views on organizations and their functioning. As a matter of fact, this body of knowledge consists of views that have gained a certain common acceptance. We could refer to them as a general organization theory. The general acceptance of new views is closely related – as we have seen in the previous chapters – with both their validity and their actuality. The opinions of Taylor, Fayol and those of Peters and Waterman, were apparently actual to a high degree; they were practically immediately added to the body of knowledge. The views of Weber, however, got little approval in his own time; they became actual in the years after World War II.

Validity and Actuality

We call opinions that do not reach the state of general acceptance private theories. We saw an example of these kind of theories in the views of Parker Follett that disappeared in the mist of history. A special case are the views of Deming. These views, already formulated in the years 1930, found only limited acceptance in business. They became, however, very actual in rebuilding the Japanese industry and, around 1980, in the United States when competition from Japan was felt. Since then Total Quality Control has also been added to our body of knowledge.

The statement that certain views on organizations must be seen as private theories does not say anything about their validity and maybe more about the way in which they take advantage of or supply an answer to things that are seen as actual questions. A clue to the question of a more general acceptance of certain opinions may be found in the way they are discussed in the specialist journals or conferences.

All this is meant to say that the body of knowledge is not a clearly defined field where specialists agree on basics and principles. In what we have called the general organization theory, opinions remain that are not or have hardly been evaluated in the light of new research. That gives contributors the possibility and opportunity to develop their own set of opinions on organization theory. It is difficult to value these opinions and ascertain whether they contribute to the scientific object of organization theory. Let us take a more elaborate look at the problem of line and staff.

The Problem of Line and Staff

At the time Scientific Management Movement got her biggest successes (between 1910 and 1940) management was confronted with ever growing numbers of employees and specialties. Horizontal and vertical differentiation thrived.

What also grew was the number of specialists at the higher levels of the organization. That growth was a direct result of changes in the environment as we saw before. The availability of new knowledge, new materials, and new technologies forced the management of organizations to take into account the new developments and to incorporate them in their production processes.

Outside the organizations and on a governmental level, new laws and regulations became necessary. Management had to consider whether the new regulations had practical consequences for their organizations. The complexity of the laws, whether it was about tax collection or reducing environmental effects, forced organizations to obtain the necessary knowledge.

This might be seen as a new phenomenon – though not the phenomenon itself was new but rather its magnitude – that resulted in the question: how do we have to describe the relation between the new specialists (the staff) and the executional part of the organization (the line). The concept of line and staff was introduced by Harrington Emerson and derived from the military organization.

Two principles dominated the discussion: the unity of command that was propagated by Fayol (in Dutch literature generally used as basic principle) and the idea that staff (specialists) were assigned to the management top and only had an advisory authority in that direction. As McGregor puts it:

The staff expert should have no authority over any part of the line organization, nor should he take any action that will interfere with line management's performances of its role.

But the world is not that simple. Again McGregor: *These conceptions are accepted as sound theory by a fair proportion of managements, but practice and theory do not always coincide.*

In the years 1960 it was clear that this purity in the doctrine resulted in permanent tensions between staff and line. According to Urwick:

While business has adopted the words staff and line from military terminology, it has shown insufficient insight into the realities those terms are used to describe. In consequence there has been almost endless confusion and conflict about the part that so-called "staff" positions are supposed to play in business organizations. Definitions of "staff" given by authorities of business management often tend to be vague, contradictory and lacking in precision. The setting up of staff positions in practice has too frequently been accompanied by disputes about competence and authority, which have often led to the discrediting, if not the dismissal of, able and enthusiastic younger executives.

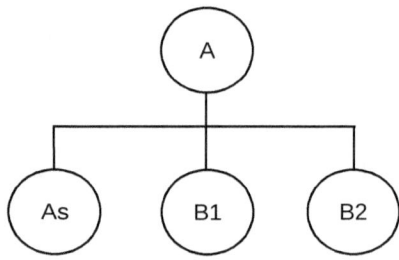

Fig. 5 The specialist role

The relationship between staff and line put a pressure on the behavior of the staff personnel. McGregor says: *It is now perhaps clear that the use of authority in the usual, reductive sense by the staff expert is an ineffective way of inducing behavior changes directed toward healthier human relations*[58]*... The line administration of personnel policies is a complex task in which the "how" is far more important than the "what". The correct "how", depending as it does upon a*

58 McGregor,

sound philosophy and upon the attitudes-behind-the-act, is rarely, if ever, induced by threats or punishment.

Wilfred Brown thought these answers were too vague and free of obligations. According to his opinion, the discussion about line and staff is caused by a lack of conceptual clarity about the content of the work that is done in business.[59] His analysis brings him to the conclusion that specialist advises not only are felt like orders, but also must be interpreted as such.

In Fig 5 As is a specialist to A in any specialty. B1 and B2 are employees and accountable to A for all decisions necessary to realize production and to maintain losses at a minimum. But As is accountable towards A for introducing new methods of production. If As as a colleague of B1 and B2 only can give advice that can be ignored, he cannot fulfill his accountability towards A and his specialty is spilled. Brown says that this situation can be filled in as follows:

- As is responsible for advising A in one specialist field.
- A appraises As's advice; he can talk about it with B1 and B2, etc. and then decides on his policy.
- A holds As responsible for realizing his (A 's) policy by B1 and B2.
- To be able to fulfill this responsibility, As gets the authority to give orders to B1 and B2 as long as these orders are within the limits of A 's policy. As gets staff authority.

Botter (Botter, 1985) was of the opinion that Brown at this point broke the unity of command. But Brown was not the only one. Kampfraath showed that the relations between employees at different levels and in different roles, in many cases, can be described appropriately by distinguishing between a hierarchical

---

59 Brown, 1971, 113.

boss, a discipline boss and a task boss relationship.[60] In other textbooks similar distinctions are made.[61]

These views that are founded on practical experience are not accepted just like that by writers on organization theory. For instance, Keuning and Eppink[62] say: *The staff is at the service of the line and has only advising authority.* And so we see that the opinion of Emerson from the beginning of the 20th century is still found in the general organization theory though it is clear that in practice his views are inadequate in large organizations.

The consultant doesn't bother very much about these discussions. He will choose whatever seems to fit best into the problem he has to solve. We see that consultants use opinions that do not appear in the leading textbooks.

Emerging of New Contributions

In the preceding chapters we have seen in what way the environment was influencing the emergence of new contributions to the organization theory. We have attributed the contributions to the people that had an important role in putting these contributions into words. In this we follow what is usual. However, we have to realize that a sketch of the environment is not enough to explain the behavior or the opinions of the writers. The real issue is to show why certain opinions emerged or flourished in a specific period.

Comparing Organizations

It is common practice in doing research on organizations to compare organizations at a certain time. Kast and Rosenzweig

---

60 Kampfraath, 1981, 67.
61 Botter, 1985, 184.
62 Keuning, 1983, 118.

devote a chapter to what they call comparative analysis. The purpose of such an analysis is to determine whether our body of knowledge (organization theory) has general characteristics and whether management capabilities are transferable over the borders of organizations and institutions. By comparative analysis organizations can be matched on a number of dimensions in their reactions to the conditions under which they work.[63]

Lammers, too, in what is called his opus magnum propagates the comparison of organizations at the same time.[64] Much of our knowledge and opinions of organizations came into being in this way, as is demonstrated by the studies of Woodward, Lawrence and Lorsch and Peters and Waterman. One common property of all these studies is that they consider and accept the conditions and structure of society as data. That is plausible. All organizations that are involved in a comparative study function in the same societal context. And not only that: views and behavior of managers and their co-workers are very well understood by the researchers who do their research in that same environment. As a result of this way of working, the results of the research are also isolated from the environment. Or the results of the research are presented without any reference to the environment in which they may be applied. Comparative analysis of organizations apparently is not the most appropriate way to demonstrate the influence of change in environmental conditions on organizations.

Expanding Theory

The fact that changing views in theory do not have the same impact on all organizations and come about under different

---

63 Kast, 1974, 125.
64 Lammers, 1997, 125.

conditions in different cultures causes new theories to spread only gradually. Therefore, new theories do not simply replace older ones, but they are added more or less as in Fig 6.

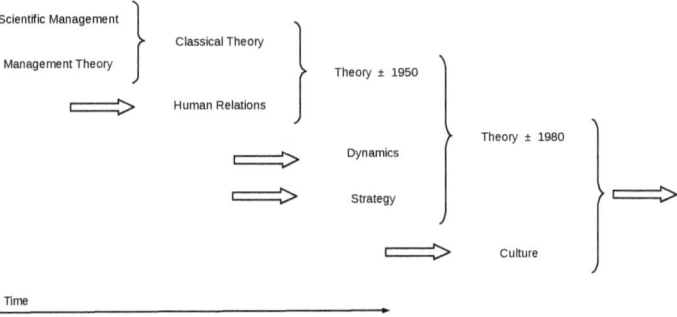

Fig.6 Expanding theory

Moreover, the fact that existing theory is not replaced as a whole means that work on the existing theory or parts of it will be continued. So we see at about 1980 – under influence of the Japanese 'threat' – an upheaval of the ideas of Deming, a whole school working out his ideas. We could speak here of a refinement of what the pioneers contributed. A good example is long term planning. The discussion started with the relatively modest book of Ansoff (Corporate Strategy) and grew into a large amount of literature that can hardly been overlooked. New terms emerge like Strategic Management, Company Development, etc.

Another aspect of theory development nowadays is that new theories are no longer the work of one man, but the result of many contributions in an international discussion. An example is the development of chain management that originated in the Wageningen approach (see chapter 5) of governing the flow of goods and which resulted in a separate journal (Journal on Chain Management), filled with contributions from everywhere over the world.

Conclusion

Many theories that are part of and make up organization theory have only limited actuality because:

- The big differentiation in organizations they have to be applied to.
- The conditions under which they are valid are not always clear.
- The way in which the theory expands leaves room for what we called here private theories.

7. Organization Theory: What is it all about

Changes in Organizations

We have seen how in the course of history, the five groups of environmental variables we introduced in chapter 2 have changed production possibilities and production processes completely. In chapter 3 we demonstrated how the superfluous availability of raw materials and markets, the lack of infrastructure and institutional restraints in the United States led to thinking on a scale that was impossible in Europe. Already on the World Exhibition of 1854 the United States showed a threshing machine that belittled the largest machines in Europe.[65]

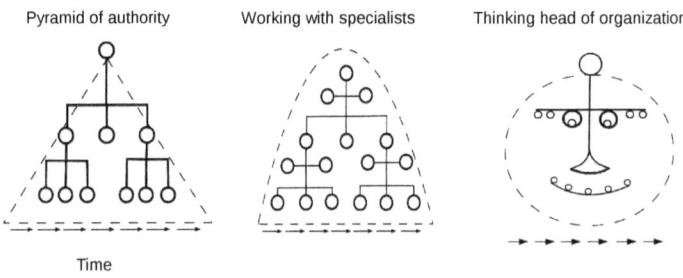

Fig.7 From pyramid of authority to thinking head

Moreover, the existing infrastructure, the national borders and, because of the national borders, the limited quantities of raw

---

65 Brogan, 1985, 387.

materials and markets in Europe caused organizations to produce on a much smaller scale.

In chapter 4 we have seen how structure and functioning of organizations grew more and more complex as a result of new laws, new tasks and functions and new technologies. But the structural characteristics of the market changed only gradually. And, thanks to the dominant position of the United States on the global markets, production could still be organized on a scale much larger than that of other countries.

At the time the theories of chapter 5 came about, a number of changes had emerged through which the advantages of scale of the United States seemed to become less important. The most important products from this period didn't need factories to be that big and were no longer tied to a specific place. They became, however, more and more knowledge intensive. The knowledge incorporated into the new technologies became an important factor. Toffler[66] speaks of a power shift.

The changes in the structure of organizations as a result of changes in the environment can be drawn as in Fig 7. The organization with its more or less military outlook changes slowly into the thinking head of the present day. Or more concretely we see:

- the shift from homework to factory production (in certain branches of industry);
- the emergence of new kinds of businesses and new branches;
- the growth of organizations in personnel as much as in volume of trade;
- the coming into being of new functions and specialties in organizations;

---

66 Toffler, 1991.

- the replacement of earlier sources of energy – water, wind and human labor – by steam and oil and electricity;
- the replacement by machines of labor that rested on human skills
- the growth of administrative organizations;
- the emergence of new jobs and technical knowledge;
- the introduction of means to take over the governing of machines;
- the introduction of the computer that replaces administrative labor and can be used to gradually take over governing processes.

Changes in Theory

Organization theory was built on the contributions of practice-oriented people who tried to generalize their knowledge from experience and people who sought a more theoretical approach. Looking over those contributions from a historical point of view, we can see a shift in the topics that are of interest. This shift also has its roots in the changing conditions of society. We will look at a few of these topics at some length.

Decreasing Attention for Efficiency

The Scientific Management Movement was strongly focused on the efficiency of production processes. That was important where human effort had an important bearing on productivity and quality. Important aspects of the efficiency of handling material were standardized conditions, improvement of methods and the experience of the skilled laborer. The experience of the skilled laborer was very important in series and mass production. Research showed that the time per unit decreased with 20% when doubling the number of items produced (the learning curve).[67]

---

67 De Jong, 1959.

In newer machines, designed to replace human labor, efficiency and quality were incorporated into the design. Therefore, the learning curve had a smaller influence on production time.

The influence of the employee on quantity and quality of production decreased further when it became possible to replace the governing of machines by machines. In the years 60 of the 20th century it was already clear that the growth of production was no longer caused by the efficiency of the laborers, but by the growth of stock of capital goods. The capital content of production rose continuously. The task of the people working in industry shifted more and more into the direction of care that machines should run without interruption.

While human physical labor slowly disappeared out of the production process, intellectual labor flourished. For intellectual labor it is not so easy to apply the usual measures of efficiency (result/costs). The application of techniques to improve working methods was also less easy in the case of mind processes. People who occupied themselves nevertheless with the efficiency of mind labor tried to find the solution in time management.[68]

More Attention for Processes

Process diagrams and process analysis belonged to the standard tools of the Scientific Management Movement. The process diagram could be used to look for improvements of methods. In most cases improvement was obtained by eliminating unnecessary transports and unnecessary delays. At the same time, the process diagram drew attention to the coherence between related processes, because the output from one process was used as input for another. Optimal flow requires careful tuning of processes.

---

68 Goedhart, 1973.

Another cause for the growing interest for processes can be found in the large scale companies in the chemical industry. In these companies, raw materials – often oil and coal – were dissected in a number of steps and processed into new products. The quality of the output of these processes was determined by the quality of the input from an earlier step in the process. Control and steering of the different steps is fundamental. The process diagram and analysis remained important in the layout of new processes and new buildings for companies. They got a new impetus when computer programs were introduced. The growing interest for processes after 1990 seems to be caused by:

- The growing critical attitude of consumers who are prepared to buy new products, but look more for an acceptable combination of price, functionality and quality;
- The growing competition from countries in Asia like China, Japan, Korea, and India that forces a rethinking of the way of producing goods. And so we don't speak any longer off mass production but of mass customization. This phenomenon, already dominant in the car industry, leads to the situation in which the product will only be constructed after the consumer has selected his own item.

In organization theory we find the results, for instance, in the opinions on networking, chain management and modular organization, opinions that all concentrate on processes. In the views about reengineering the corporation, the network is not only seen as a phenomenon inside one organization but also as something that facilitates the cooperation between companies.

Growing Attention for Motivation and Group Behavior.

There are a few opinions in classical theory that have drawn only little attention. One of these notions was the idea of Taylor that management and worker have a common interest and thus have to cooperate extensively. It was an idea that was not heartily welcomed in a society in which the contrast between leader and worker was the basis on which the unions thrived. But in the course of history we meet this opinion time and again. We mentioned it already with Parker Follett (around 1930), Deming (around 1950) and also by Peters and Waterman (around 1980).

Growing competition and changing market positions forced companies to look for ways to induce their workers to perform better. We already saw that new dynamics in international competitive relations around 1960 led to the awareness that organizational change had to be seen as a normal phenomenon. The experience that large organizational changes provoke big resistance inside the organization induced management to look for other approaches. Moreover the years 60 of the 20th century in the United States as well as elsewhere were a period in which authority had lost much of its automatic legitimacy. It was a time in which race discrimination led to extreme outbursts and in which a new feminist wave passed through society.

In that situation the idea of Kurt Lewin that proposed a process in three steps (unfreeze - change - freeze) became popular. Kurt Lewin proposed a strategy of discrete steps of change so that after a change the company could go on for a prolonged period of time. Lewin's approach concentrated the attention on the process of change and, more specifically, on how management and workers together would implement the changes. In the following years many process-oriented approaches were presented under the name organization development. In the Netherlands the model of the NPI was popular.

More Attention for Leadership

Fayol is considered to be the first to regard management as a task separate from other tasks in the company. At the time of Fayol, ownership and leadership in the company were practically synonyms. The fact that Fayol made a distinction can be seen as a sign of change in society and organizations. That change had different aspects. The growth of companies, improved means of transport and the need to increase turnover brought entrepreneurs in contact with new markets and other enterprises. They made it clear that for an efficient allocation of people and resources, other capabilities were needed than could be obtained by only heritage and family relations. At the same time, growing companies needed more money for investments and often more than the owner could supply. And so ownership and leadership were separated gradually. New legal forms of organization were introduced to enable this change. And this made it also clear there was a growing need for another kind of leadership.

Forty years after Fayol, his view that managers had to have certain capabilities had become an obvious fact. Even so far that the question came up as to whether education and management training were not enough. In the introduction of his well known book in the Netherlands, Van der Schroeff elaborates on the question of whether leadership is an art (that is: inborn) or a craft (something that can be learned). Van der Schroeff states that in the Netherlands people tend to think: "leaders are born not made", whereas in America the slogan : "managers are made, not born" is popular. (Schroeff, 1968: 15). According to Van der Schroeff, both opinions are in a way true. At the same time in the United States, Allen wrestles with the same choice between art and craft but without making clear his own position. He confines himself to the necessary knowledge and skills of the leader. (Allen, 1964: 106).

Pfiffner and Sherwood[69] point to the fact that the personality of the leader can be crucial. They use an example from the Second World War: General Omar Bradley was confronted with the problem of commanding the 90th infantry division. This division performed so badly in the operations in Normandy that Bradley's staff wanted the division disbanded. Bradley, however, thought that as for the men one division was not better than another, but that the differences lay in the competence and the leadership of the commanding officers. He assigned a new commanding officer who implemented 16 changes in the organization of 16,000 men. His successor inherited one of the most able-bodied divisions of the allied front.

The opinion that the personality of the leader can be decisive must have many supporters in our day when we look at the way in which competent leaders switch from one organization to another. The same opinion is heard in politics. 'Politics is only about persons'.[70] But nevertheless everybody seems to be convinced that even the competent leader needs a sound education and a broad knowledge of everything that concerns leadership.

More Attention for Steering

In chapter 2, we said that the leader in large organizations has evolved into one or more complex steering organs. Leadership of the organization became more and more an abstraction. The manager merged into the steering organ. The steering task can also be denoted as governing. And when organizations become

---

69 Pfiffner & Sherwood, 1966, 339.
70 Velde, 2002, Introduction.

more complex, the controllability becomes more and more important. Steering as an abstract process got an important impact from developments in technology. Technology made it possible to let the steering of machines be taken over by technical tools and this helped the development of cybernetics. Apart from that, systems theory offered ideas and concepts for the steering of systems. Several of these ideas (input, output, and feedback, for instance) have become part of our daily language. It might be thought that going from the steering from machines to the steering of organizations would be a small step. But this is deceptive. Systems theory was meant to bring a large number of phenomenon under one common denominator by calling it a system. Boulding (1956), one of the founders of systems theory, distinguished nine levels of system which were hierarchically coupled. Every level in the hierarchy contained the properties of the lower level plus something more. Boulding put organizations that are social systems in level 8. The steering principles offered by cybernetics and models that are used by them only reach level three: the level of cybernetic systems. But nevertheless these developments stimulate the attention for the steering of systems.

Recently a new word has been introduced in the world of steering and governing of organizations: corporate governance. The meaning of this expression is not clearly defined (internet encyclopedia Encycogov gives six definitions to indicate its significance). OECD uses this description: *Corporate Governance is the system by which business corporations are directed and controlled. The corporate governance structure specifies the distribution of rights and responsibilities among different participants in the corporation, such as the board, managers, shareholders and other stakeholders, and spells out the rules and procedures for making decisions on corporate affairs. By doing this it also provides the structure through which the company objectives are set, and the means of attaining those objectives and monitoring performance.* (OECD, cited by Encycogov).

The other definitions are less elaborate but most definitions point to the growing importance that is attached to the cooperation between shareholders and the boards of corporations, more specifically, in the field of financial responsibility and control. There are also indications that in corporations where the relationship between shareholders and the board are more democratic, profitability of the corporation rises. The expression "corporate governance" has become popular in a short time and is used in information about corporations as a point of reference.

More Attention to Strategy and Competition

In discussions over organizations few words have been abused as much as the word planning. And yet certain fundamental notions are obvious. Who wants to go from one place to another whether it is real movement or metaphorical does well to determine:

- what is the situation he is starting from;
- where his goal is and what obstacles he might meet on his way to his goal;
- in what way he thinks he can reach his goal;
- what resources he needs and how he can obtain them.

Or it is sensible to make a plan that brings him to his goal. For individuals and small groups it is not necessary to put the plan on paper in a formal way. He who made the plan knows, by heart, all necessary activities and the way they are linked together. But things change when the planning concerns the activities of a number of people and the activities they are involved in. In those cases, it may be necessary to formalize the plan and make the needed agreements. So in a plan we always see the following characteristics:

a. There is a known starting situation.

b. There is a known goal.

c. The route to the goal is clear and well defined.

In this context, planning means the care that the activities under c. are carried out with optimal efficiency. Determining the goal does not belong to the planning of the activities. We are aware of the fact that we take position in a frequently held discussion. After all, it is possible that the activities, that should bring us from a. to b., are part of a larger set of activities for which the plan had to be made, so that our goal is the outcome of the larger plan. This is a situation that happens often and that nearly automatically gets the planners involved in discussions on goals. That caused a gradual shift in the meaning of the word planning.

We have already seen that it is important to know how much time and resources are needed to realize the different activities of a plan. In many cases it is difficult to ascertain this data with any degree of certainty so that execution of a plan always carries the risk of exceeding the available time or resources. And yet in the years 1950 - 1960, planning proved to be a big success in realizing projects with a single goal and dedicated resources, even more when PERT (Programming, Evaluation and Review Technique, one of the eldest techniques of network planning) was introduced. The showpiece – was said – is the use of PERT in controlling the building of the Polaris rocket. Several estimates have been made about the degree in which the building was sped up because of the use of PERT; these estimates vary from 18 months to three years and of course there is no way to confirm any of them.[71]

The success of planning, combined with a general feeling that the future of society could be created, stimulated the feeling that possibilities of planning could be extended limitlessly. And here we enter the domain of strategic planning. Strategic planning differs in a number of respects from the planning of activities for single goals:

- Time horizon is most of the time farther.
- More than one goal (or a more complex goal) has to be accomplished.
- The goals are less clearly defined.
- The way in which the goals can be reached are less well known.

As a result of this, strategic planning is surrounded with many more uncertainties than project planning and control of the processes under strategic planning are more difficult and riskier.

Though literature on strategic planning was very successful, results were often disappointing. Maybe because the expectations of the planners were hardly realistic. Mintzberg[72] elaborates in detail on the expectations and disappointments of strategic planning. He also deals in detail with all the pitfalls planners fell into over time.

Notwithstanding the many handicaps, policy makers and decision makers keep busy with strategic planning. Rightly so, one is tempted to say, for the alternative is not very clear. But where they need to convince representatives or stockholders to get their plans approved, they are tempted to present a higher degree of certainty than they can realize.

---

71 Battersby, 1967, 7.
72 Mintzberg, 1994.

Conclusion

In this chapter we have shown that the focus of organization theory has shifted throughout the years. We have seen also that the shift is largely induced by changes in organizations and in their environment. As key factors we saw:

- Growing size and complexity of organizations.
- Rising prosperity of employees.
- Rising level of education of employees.
- Change in technology.
- Changing market relations.
- Change of norms and values in society.

And so we see that developments in theory accompany those in the societal environment of organizations as well as contributors.

8. So how do we go on?

In this chapter we use our findings of the former chapters but we are leaving the beaten track. Until now we tried with hindsight to explain what was new in organization theory. We saw in a number of cases what was new was an extension of existing theory, but also that the new views mirrored changing views on parts of existing theories. In both cases we could link the new views with change in the environment. In this chapter we will try and examine whether change in our environment can give us indications for further developments in organization theory. Therefore we will look first at the developments in the environmental factors as we see them.

The Environment

Relevant Developments in Technology

Developments in technology dominate our world. Therefore, it is important for our reasoning to see if technology shows developments that are important for the shape and functioning of organizations and for the development of the theory. We don't have the pretensions that we could appreciate developments in technology rightly. That would ask for a study of another character and scope. But maybe that is not necessary at all. After all we have already seen that change in technology and techniques are reflected only marginally in theory. Or even stronger: when we look at opinions in organization theory we see they only seldom refer to changes in technology and even if they do it is only indirect.

Therefore we will point to a few relevant developments of technology in an abstract way and while doing so, we see three trends: growing complexity, more mutual dependencies and more integration.

Growing Complexity

The growing complexity, that is a result of technological development, has different consequences for management.

- A large number of interdependent factors have to be overseen and evaluated in decisions about the desirability to use the new technical possibilities. As a result of this we see:
- The need to follow technological change in many fields and keep knowledge about these changes in the own firm. This requires a broad knowledge management.
- At the same time it requires a kind of steering that - despite complexity – enables the organization to choose the right moment to introduce the new technical possibilities.

Enhanced Integration

Technical integration means that different steps in production processes are coupled. In many cases and as a result of this coupling, the steering of the processes is included in the processes. Examples of this development are found everywhere: from the fully automated construction lines in the car industry to the full integration of text, image and sound in the modern communication apparatus. For management this means that the steering of processes is elevated to a higher level: the design of the steering of the production processes.

Growing Dependency

The complex and integrated reality of our times creates several interrelated kinds of dependency:

- Dependency between the stability and the security of systems. Stability can be seen as the degree to which a system is prone to failure as a result of technical errors or lack of skills or maliciousness.
- Dependency between the knowledge required for the maintenance, the development and implementation of systems; the continued availability of this knowledge is of the utmost importance for the competitive capacity of the organization.

These kinds of dependency are interrelated and together represent a new element in the complexity of society.

Economic Developments

Most of the time economic development is equated to growth of production, growth of (international) trade and increasing prosperity. We see here the same factors of growing complexity, integration and dependency that we saw in technological development, albeit in other fields. But apart from these trends, that influence every country, we see two dominant trends: globalization and a shift of economic focus.

Globalization

Country borders were never a big obstruction for large companies. Branches and takeovers offered the possibility to enlarge their own market and also made it possible – by making use of the difference in factory costs – to optimize their own cost structure. These enterprises, however, have a special problem as a result of the differences in organization culture in the different branches.

For smaller companies, that until now have been operating mostly locally, globalization often brings the necessity to step into the adventure of operating on a foreign market. In many cases they will have to cooperate with other – foreign – companies. And often the (legal) form of many of these cooperations (alliances) must still be developed.

Shift of Economic Center of Gravity

The cooperation of the countries of the European Union has created an internal market that now is nearly one and a half times that of the United States. When we look at the new growing markets in fast-developing countries like China, India, Brazil and Russia, we see a shift in the flow of trade, of markets and production possibilities.

For the individual company this means competition that never existed and, at the same time, possibilities in creating new markets. This requires an orientation on other cultures and languages, that will intensify in the years to come.

Markets

Technological development and globalization lead to ever new markets and market segments. An interesting example is the development of the Internet as a global marketplace. Through the Internet, companies get access to consumers all over the world, which creates also the possibility to sell very specific products for which possibilities on the local market are too small. On the other hand, the Internet has become an important competitor for companies on the local market.

As a matter of fact, the Internet as a market place is not only important as an output market but it also becomes of growing importance on the input markets. Think for example of application and recruitment through the Internet.

Markets do not change only because of changing technology. The structure of the labor market, for instance, is changing considerably as a result of the gradually aging population. The causes that are working globally are sufficiently known: better medical care and decreasing marital fertility, processes that are related to increasing prosperity and conscious population policy.

Against this background of rising societal costs of an aging (and in many countries inactive) population and the necessity to maintain knowledge and experience, choices will have to be made that go beyond the possibilities of the individual company. But it is inevitable that the individual organization will have to accommodate internally to these developments.

Institutions

The developments we pointed out require mutual agreements and control. To regulate and control societal processes new and ever more complex rules are necessary. These rules require a network of institutions. Which is an additional factor in the growing complexity of the environment that confronts management.

Locally, nationally and internationally there is a continuous pressure to reduce the number of rules. In practice this proves to be a very difficult problem that can only be solved (maybe) in the long run. In the meantime, organizations will have to learn to live with the burden of – as they experience it – a world of abundant laws and rules.

The Effect of Cultural Differences

Cultures in organizations like the ones in societies change only very slowly. Cultures govern the relations between people in a society. We see how globalization puts pressure on the different cultures. We see processes of mixing cultures, as well as processes in which cultures collide and look for confrontation.

For managers of international operating companies this is not a new situation. But other managers will be more and more confronted with different cultures within their companies. Intercultural management is a problem that grows more important by the day.

Change in Organizations

A changing environment leads to change in the structure of organizations. In the preceding chapters we didn't pay attention to the opinions of Juran. His book *Managerial Breakthrough* appeared in 1964, more or less at the same time as the theories of Ansoff and those of Lawrence and Lorsch. In 1996, Juran's book was reprinted in Dutch (title: Doorbraak in Management). Juran argues that the manager of any organization has two important tasks: he has to create a breakthrough in every field of management and he has to take care that daily business is attended to and that daily performance is of constant and good quality. In internationally operating organizations and especially in the service-providing sector, these two tasks seem to grow into two separate parts of the organization with also two different kinds of employees:

- Employees that are occupied with innovation and breakthrough of existing patterns; they are mostly highly educated people with an open and international orientation.
- Employees providing the direct services; these are people with a limited education, mostly recruited from the local market with a working attitude that fits in a bureaucratic system.

The distance between those two parts of the organization slowly grows but confronts the management with a growing problem of coordination.

On the other hand when we look at the organizational structure of new internet companies like Google they look strikingly familiar, with their division in sections, departments or divisions. Maybe organizational change in our digital age will not be so disruptive as we think.

Effect on Theory

What does all this mean for organization theory? How do we handle the developments we mentioned here: growing complexity related to increasing prosperity and at the same time mixing or confronting cultures? Or – in relation to the increasing prosperity – how do we handle the growing use of scarce resources and growing dependencies? Is there room for an organization theory that helps structuring individual organizations, their functioning and change?

In chapter 6, we have shown how through the years, new elements were added to the already existing body of knowledge, but hardly any elements were discarded. We may assume that this picture will remain the case in the time to come. After all, organizations exist of people that will not change fundamentally, not even when the number of aging people grows relatively. So maybe it will be enough to develop add-ons or modifications to existing theories that will enable people, managers and employees, to handle the yet-to-come developments as well as possible. When we see things correctly, theory has to deal with a few problems that we call the *challenge to theory building.*

New Models for Task Building and Work Organization

An aging population forces organizations to accommodate important changes in individual organizations. New models for building tasks are needed as well as new kinds of workfloor organization. The many changes in the environment and the internal changes ask for a flexible approach to the working situation that makes it possible to use and keep the experience and knowledge of older workers.

Theory from China and India?

We have seen that the fast growth of the Japanese economy between 1975 and 1985 led to a new appreciation of quality management. What may be the contribution of the fast growing economies of China and India? The Olympic Games in Beijing were an impressive demonstration of Chinese power to organize big events. What can we learn from this demonstration? As always, looking into the future is a risky business. But literature on China booms. What does it show?

Experiences of companies in China are controversial. Quality management requires a strong discipline of all members in the organization which seems to be a characteristic of Japanese culture. Such a discipline does not exist in China, maybe because the culture in this enormous country is too diverse. And yet the great performance in most sports requires a concentration and a discipline that could only be reached by a strong and central government that sees this good performance as a goal. The lack of discipline as a cultural asset makes the need for principles less evident. But in China a few Confucian principles still prevail: respect for the family and the elderly people and the need for relatives to get ahead. These principles give organizations a strong hierarchy and at the same time many informal contacts. Informal organizations still flourish in China.

The informal organization is a concept that emerged in the years thirty of the 20th century as a byproduct of the Hawthorn Research. It was noted that there was not only a formal organization (the organization that was described in organization charts and handbooks), but also an informal organization that is inevitable, and most of the time necessary, to keep the formal organization going. The informal organization is founded on the individual relations between people as a result of their interacting. In western literature it is usually assumed that an informal organization needs not to be seen as negative, as long as it functions as a valuable addition to the formal organization. The informal organization, however, can, under certain conditions, be disastrous for the formal organization. In a country where the informal organization plays an important role in business as it does in China, we may assume that contributions from China will reflect the importance of informal organization.

Developments in India seem less spectacular than those in China. But the takeovers of French steel giant Arcelor by Mittal Steel and of Corus by Tata make clear that India has changed very fast in recent years.

Compared to China, India has the advantage of a foundation of legal and financial institutions ready to participate in world economy, along with a younger workforce. On the other hand, in India – the world's largest democracy - decision making is slow, making improvement of the infrastructure extremely difficult. And yet, India is already the fifth largest investor in the UK and India's economy is expected to outstrip UK's in the next decade.

So there is every reason to watch developments in India closely and see what kind of new organizations will emerge and what contribution India has to offer towards organization theory. A few developments are worth being noted. To appreciate what is happening in India, we have to look at traditional production processes in the west. In the car industry, for example, cars are designed, constructed, assembled and shipped to dealers and local vendors. The system Tata is developing skips in this chain of processes: the assembly and the dealers. Assembly and sale come together at the local vendor. We can see here how the production process is being redesigned in India. And how the roles of local vendor and production factory may change.

Attention for Alliances

One way to enjoy the advantages of scale and flexibility and yet avoid the difficulties that are inherent to fusion or takeovers, is making alliances. Alliances have the additional advantage that partners stay independent and, moreover, the alliance can be made for shorter or longer periods. That's why alliances may provide a larger range of solutions for organizational problems.

Alliances are already so common that contributors to the theory have become interested.

Meta Steering

Many decision processes, together with the accompanying checks on the results, become larger and more complex. Consider, for example, the process of realizing a large project (large buildings, subway lines etc.) or the investments of large corporations. One of the causes for the complexity of the decision making process is the number of participants involved and the many aspects that have to be considered. Because such projects have important financial consequences and consequences in time, decision making processes and evaluation processes must be carefully structured. After that they must be carefully executed and checked.

The following example shows the importance of an active structuring of the decision making processes. After examination of the way in which the redesign of station squares came into being, remarkable differences appeared in the time the processes took. In those cases where no measures were taken regarding the way the decision making process was structured (that is, where the realization process had been left to itself), the design took considerably more time – up to a few years – than in those cases where special measures were taken. Processes where the decision making process had been structured, took about one and a half year. In the process that was fastest in realization, the NS (the Dutch railway Company) and the community involved each had assigned an official. Together the two officials had to make sure that the different parties involved in the process were called in on time and in the right way. Moreover, the two of them were responsible together for the progress of the decision making process.

A station square is – seen from the point of view of building – not a very impressive product. But it is a product which deals with many interests. For instance, to list some: the interests of the railway company, the community, the mail, local and regional transport, local trades people and the business community that may be interested in building hotels, offices and conference rooms, etc.

Direction of the steering process (meta steering) is not only important in individual organizations and projects. Interfering with the conditions of the decision making process makes it possible to obtain important societal effects.

An Integrative Paradigm

Organization theory presents itself as an interdisciplinary science. This science lacks, however, a clear paradigm that enables the integration of contributions of other disciplines. Cases are used to explain to students how integration can take place, but these cases lack the supporting paradigm. Here lies an important challenge for those contributors that really think in an interdisciplinary manner.

Finally

Organizations determine in large our society, so everybody gets in touch with or is involved in organizations. Therefore, it may be useful to understand the history and background of thinking about organizations. We have drawn a few lines through the thoughts about organizations – organization theory. One line is about growing complexity of organizations and its consequences; one line was about the need for cooperation between the different levels in an organization, and one line was about the increase of requirements that are imposed on the steering and governing of organizations.

We hope that this book will contribute to a better understanding of the organization theory and the way it is integrated in its social environment. A better understanding of what is required for a modern organization may also draw attention to the complex problems of governing of our time and the time to come. That asks for a combined effort of all contributors to the theory and much positive decisiveness of governors and politicians.

Bibliography

Allen,1964:	Allen, L. A., *Het beroep van manager*,
Spectrum,Utrecht;Antwerpen1964

Ansoff,1965:	Ansoff, H.I., *Corporate Strategy*, McGraw-
Hill,New York1965

Battersby,1966:	Battersby, A., *Netwerk*, Het Spectrum,Utrecht;
Antwerpen1966

Beer,1979:	Beer, Stafford, *The Heart of Enterprise*, John
Wiley and Sons,Chichester1979.

Bennis, 1974:	Bennis, Warren, *Organisation development:
its nature, origins, and prospects*, Addison-Wesley, 1969.

Berman, 2000:	Berman, Morris, *The Twilight of American
Culture*, W.W.Norton&Company, Inc,New York2004

Birnie,1965:	Birnie, A., *Economische geschiedenis van
Europa van 1760-1939*, Het Spectrum,Utrecht; Antwerpen1965

Botter,1985:	Botter, prof.ir C.H., *Industrie en Organisatie*,
Kluwer/NIVE,Deventer1985

Brogan,1985:	Brogan, Hugh, *The Penguin History of the
United States of America*, Penguin Books,London1985

Brown,1971:	Brown, Wilfred, *Organization*,
Heinemann,London1971

Dopuch,1974:	Dopuch, Nicholas; Jacob G, Birnberg; Joel
Demski, *Cost Accounting*, Harcourt Brace Jovanovich, Inc,New
York; etc1974

Drucker, 1996:	Drucker, Peter, *Introduction* in P.Graham (ed):
Mary Parker Follett, Prophet of Management,
Harvard,Boston1996

Drucker,1957:	Drucker, Peter F., *Management in de Praktijk*,
J. H. de Bussy,1970.

Durkheim, 1893: Durkheim, E., *La division sociale du travail*, ,
1893

Fayol,1949:   Fayol, Henri, *General and Industrial Mana-
gement*, Sir Isaac Pitman & Sons,London1949
Girard,2000: Girard, B., *Une histoire des theories de manage-
ment en France de 1800 à 1940*, 2000,
Glasl,1975:   Glasl,F and L. de la Houssaye,
Organisatieontwikkeling in de Praktijk, Agon
Elsevier,Amsterdam1975
Goedhart,1973: Goedhart, E., *Efficiency van het denkwerk*, Het
Spectrum,Utrecht/Antwerpen1973
Hijmans,1973:   Hijmans, E., *Zestig jaar Organiseren*, Nijgh en
Van Ditmar,Rotterdam1973
Huffington, 2011, Huffington, Arianna, *Third World America*,
Broadway Paperbacks, New York 2011.
Hofstede,1994: Hofstede, Geert, *Cultures and Organizations*,
Harper Collins,London1994
Ishikawa, 1985: Ishikawa, Kauro, *What is Total Quality
Control*, Prentice-Hall,Englewood Cliffs, N.J.1985
Johnson,1999:   Johnson, Paul, *A History of the American
People*, Harper Perennial,New York1999
Kampfraath,1969:   Kampfraath, prof. drs. A. A., *Organi-
satie van het Samenspel van Managers en Specialisten*, Het
Spectrum,Utrecht; Antwerpen1969
Kampfraath,1981:   Kampfraath, prof. drs. A.A. en ir W.J.
Marcelis, *Besturen en organiseren,* Kluwer,Deventer1981
Kanigel, 1997: Kanigel, Robert, *The one best Way*, Viking
(Penguin Group),New York1997
Kast,1974:   Kast, Fremont E.; James E. Rosenzweig,
Organization and Management, McGraw-Hill
Kogakusha,Tokyo1974
Keuning,1993:   Keuning, D.; D.J. Eppink, *Management en
Organisatie*, Stenfert Kroese,Leiden/Antwerpen1993
Kramer,1991:   Kramer, N.J.T.A. en J de Smit, *Systeemdenken*,
Stenfert Kroese,Leiden/Antwerpen1991

Lammers,1997: Lammers, C.J.; A.A. Mijs; W.J. van Noort, *Organisaties vergelijkenderwijs*, Het Spectrum,Utrecht/Antwerpen1997

Lawrence,1967: Lawrence, Paul R. and Jay W. Lorsch, *Organization and Environment*, Harvard University,Boston1967

Luiten,2000: Luiten van Zanden, Dr.Jan; Arthur van Riel, *Nederland, 1780-1914*, Balans,Amsterdam2000

Luiten,1997: Luiten van Zanden, J., *Een klein land in de 20e eeuw*, Het Spectrum,Utrecht/Antwerpen1997

March, 1969 March, James G, en Herbert Simon, *Organisaties,* De Bussy, Amsterdam, 1969.

Meij,1958: Meij, prof.dr. J.L.; drs.P.M.M.H.Snel, *Leerboek der Bedrijfseconomie II*, Uitgeversmaatschappij v/h G. Delwel,Den Haag1958

Mintzberg, 1994: Mintzberg, Henry, *Opkomst en ondergang van Strategische Planning*, Academic Service,Schoonhoven1994

Mintzberg,1983: Mintzberg, Henry, *Power in and around Organizations*, Prentice Hall,Englewood Cliffs, NJ1983

Nevins, 1992: Nevins, Allan; Henry Steel Commager with Jeffrey Morris, *A Pocket History of the United States,* Pocket Books,New York1992

Packard, 1963-1: Packard, Vance, *The hidden Persuaders*, Pocket Books,New York1963

Packard,1963-2: Packard, Vance, *The Wastemakers*, Pocket Books,New York1963

Graham, 1996: Parker Follett, Mary, *Mary Parker Follett, Prophet of Management*, Harvard Business School Press,Boston1996

Waterman, 1984: Peters,Thomas J. and Robert H. Waterman Jr, *In Search of Excellence*, Warner Books, Inc.,New York1984

Pfiffner,1966:   Pfiffner, John M. and Frank P. Sherwood, *Moderne organisatieleer,* Het Spectrum,Utrecht/Antwerpen1966
Propper,1993:   Propper, I.M.A.M., *Inleiding in de Organisatietheorie,* VUGA Uitgeverij,Den Haag1993
Ricardo,1971:   Ricardo, David, *On the Principles of Political Economy and Taxation,* Penguin Books ltd.,Middlesex
Roethlisberger,1939:   Roethlisberger, F. and W.J. Dickson, *Management and the Worker,* Harvard University Press,Cambridge1939
Schroeff,1968:   Schroeff, H.J. van der, *Leiding en Organisatie van het Bedrijf,* Kosmos,Amsterdam1968
Sieren,2006:   Sieren, Frank, *Der China Code,* Ullstein Taschenbuch,Berlin2006
Taylor,1913:   Taylor, Frederic Winslow, *The Principles of Scientific Management,* Harper,New York1913
Toffler,1991:   Toffler, Alvin, *Powershift,* Bantam Books,London1991
Urwick, 1949:   Urwick, L., *General and Industrial Management* (Foreword), Isaac Pitman &Sons,London1949
Urwick, 1956:   Urwick, L., *The Golden Book of Management,* Newman Neame,London1956
Velde,2002:   Velde, Henk te, *Stijlen van leiderschap,* Wereldbibliotheek,Amsterdam2002
Walter,1998:   Walter, R., *Wirtschaftsgeschichte,* Böhlau Verlag,Keulen1998
Weber,2005:   Weber, M., *Wirtschaft und Gesellschaft,* J. C. B. Mohr,Tubingen2005
Zahn,1991:   Zahn, Ernest, *Regenten, rebellen en reformatoren,* Contact,Amsterdam1991
Zinn,1995:   Zinn, Howard, *A People's History of the United States,* Harper Perennial,New York1995
Zwart,1973:   Zwart, C.J., *Gericht veranderen van Organisaties,* Lemniscaat,Rotterdam1973

De Jong,1959:   De Jong, Dr. Ir. J. R., *Bekwaamheid, seriegrootte en benodigde tijd*, Berenschot, 1959.

www.ingramcontent.com/pod-product-compliance
Lightning Source LLC
Chambersburg PA
CBHW051922170526
45168CB00001B/497